Praise for *uncluttered faith*

"Joshua Becker used to be a pastor; now he's a prophet. He is exposing one of the most dangerous idols of our day: materialism. It turns out that the stuff we own owns us. We sacrifice to get it and bow down under the weight of it. Rather than more time, money, or stuff, we need more margin, because the margins (physical, emotional, and spiritual) are where all the best things in life live. This book will be the prophetic strategy you've been longing for to finally find shalom."

—MARK E. MOORE, bestselling author of *Core 52*

"With grace and wisdom, Joshua Becker shows how decluttering our home makes space for peace and purpose. This is more than a book about owning less; it's an invitation to live with purpose. If your heart longs for peace, freedom, and a deeper faith, this book will meet you right where you are."

—ZOË KIM, founder of Raising Simple and author of *Minimalism for Families*

"I am one of the millions who have been inspired by Joshua Becker's bestselling books—teaching us to unclutter our lives to create space for more of what truly matters. In *Uncluttered Faith,* Becker invites us to take the next step, using our uncluttered lives to deepen our faith and make a lasting difference in the world around us. He meticulously lays out how our overattachment to wealth distracts us from our pursuit of God, and he provides practical steps to leverage minimalism for a life filled with not just more joy and purpose but also more impact."

—GLEN VAN PESKI, founder of Gossamer Gear and author of *Take Less. Do More.*

"*Uncluttered Faith* is a clear and compelling invitation to experience more of God by embracing less of the world. As both a friend and a colleague, I've had the privilege of watching Becker live out these truths for nearly twenty years. What he writes here is not theory but hard-won wisdom. The ways of Jesus described in these pages have brought freedom and blessing to many, and they can do the same for you."

—JOE DARAGO, executive director of The Hope Effect

"Imagine your life with less debt, less pull from consumerism, and more money for God's work. This book shows a simple way to start. As someone who has spent the last twenty years helping Christians find more money to fund their missions, I'm thrilled about the clear, biblical steps Becker lays out. I'll be pointing my students to this for years."

—BOB LOTICH, award-winning author of *Simple Money, Rich Life* and founder of SeedTime.com

"In a noisy, distracted world, *Uncluttered Faith* is a clear call to simplify and give God our best. Joshua Becker not only exposes the clutter that keeps us from Him but also gives practical, hope-filled steps to clear the way. This book is timely, practical, and deeply needed for anyone who longs for a faith that is focused and free."

—TRAVIS BROWN, former NFL quarterback and pastor at Christ's Church of the Valley

"Freeing ourselves of clutter can get us spiritually closer to our faith and our true selves. Joshua Becker has a way of keeping things clear and down-to-earth—*Uncluttered Faith* is full of the kind of wisdom that makes you stop, think, and want to live a more intentional life that allows you to focus on what truly matters: our family, faith, and friends."

—MATT PAXTON, host of *Filthy Fortunes* and *Hoarders,* and author of *Keep the Memories, Lose the Stuff*

"We often don't realize how much our overflowing calendars and closets negatively impact all parts of our lives, including our faith. In *Uncluttered Faith,* Joshua Becker calls us to unclutter and simplify, so we can focus on the most important aspects of our lives—including prioritizing people rather than possessions and finding purpose beyond a paycheck!"

—CRYSTAL PAINE, *New York Times* bestselling author, founder of MoneySavingMom.com, and host of *The Crystal Paine Show*

uncluttered faith

unclutteredfaith

Own Less, Love More, and Make an Impact in Your World

JOSHUA BECKER
WITH ERIC STANFORD

WaterBrook

WaterBrook
An imprint of the Penguin Random House Christian Publishing Group,
a division of Penguin Random House LLC
1745 Broadway, New York, NY 10019
waterbrookmultnomah.com
penguinrandomhouse.com

Italics in Scripture quotations reflect the author's added emphasis.

Library of Congress Cataloging-in-Publication Data

Names: Becker, Joshua author | Stanford, Eric other
Title: Uncluttered faith / Joshua Becker, with Eric Stanford.
Description: First edition. | [Colorado Springs, CO] : WaterBrook, [2026] |
Includes bibliographical references.
Identifiers: LCCN 2025025134 (print) | LCCN 2025025135 (ebook) |
ISBN 9780593603536 hardcover | ISBN 9780593603550 ebook
Subjects: LCSH: Christian life | Simplicity—Religious aspects—Christianity
Classification: LCC BV4501.3 .B429 2026 (print) | LCC BV4501.3 (ebook) |
DDC 248.4—dc23/eng/20250825
LC record available at https://lccn.loc.gov/2025025134
LC ebook record available at https://lccn.loc.gov/2025025135

Printed in the United States of America

1st Printing

First Edition

The authorized representative in the EU for product safety and compliance is Penguin Random House Ireland, Morrison Chambers, 32 Nassau Street, Dublin D02 YH68, Ireland. https://eu-contact.penguin.ie

BOOKMAKING TEAM: Production editor: Jessica Choi • Managing editor: Julia Wallace • Production manager: Katie Zilberman • Copy editor: Tracey Moore • Proofreaders: Bailey Utecht, Marisa Crumb

Book design by Diane Hobbing

For details on special quantity discounts for bulk purchases, contact specialmarketscms@penguinrandomhouse.com.

To my wife, Kimberly, my most precious partner in ministry for more than twenty-five years

contents

uncluttered
faith

1

The Way to Unlock God's Blessings

It was rainy when Amy Slenker-Smith[1] pulled her car into a parking spot at Target in the Washington, D.C., suburb where she lived. She cinched her raincoat closer around her, then hustled around the car to get her infant son, Zack, from the back seat so they could head into the store and buy the stuff on her list.

She'd done this same shopping excursion many times. A thirtysomething mom at the time, she worked fifty hours a week, did the daycare dash every Monday through Friday, and stopped at Target at least once a week so she could bring more stuff into her home. All in all, the actions of a typical middle-class woman.

But this day would go differently.

Over the previous months, Amy had been reevaluating her life and commitments. It had taken Amy and her husband, Steve, several years to conceive Zack. With that in mind, she had said to herself, *We worked too hard to have a child for me to just see him briefly in the mornings and put him to bed in the evenings.* So, she and Steve had begun a journey of removing the excess from their life so they could be more available for their son.

And now she found herself in the Target parking lot, raindrops wetting her long brown hair. Just as she was about to drag Zack out of his seat, she stopped and just stood beside her car, staring at the giant discount store with its red-and-white bull's-eye logo prominent on the façade.

"Suddenly it hit me: *There is nothing inside that store I truly need today*," Amy remembers. "*There is nothing that's going to add any value to my life. Even worse, it means I'll have less time at home with my husband and son.*"

So, she got back into her car and drove away, buying nothing.

From this point on, Amy was unstoppable in decluttering and de-owning everything she could. She used evenings, weekends, and Zack's nap times to do the work. Along the way she read everything she could find about living a simpler life. The process changed her entire life. Today, she is a Becker Method certified declutterer and gives advice to others at her website, Simply Enough.

"Now what I try to share with others," Amy told me, "is that your stuff, your time, and your money are heavily intertwined. I learned that I wanted to use my time and my money differently."

But Amy's story doesn't end there. Around that same time, Amy and Steve had reconnected with their faith and had begun attending church again and growing spiritually. "Minimalism freed me to become a more available mother. It also freed me to focus on my relationship with God in a different, more intentional way. We had less stuff but more God," she says.

I wonder how many Christians are like Amy on that rainy day at Target—their lives cluttered with so much stuff, so focused on buying, storing, and maintaining things, that it squelches their happiness and frustrates their purpose. My guess is that, here in the United States and in many other affluent lands, this is almost a universal problem among my fellow believers. One with *immense, incalculable costs.*

Owning more seems to be the target we're all aiming for when it comes to happiness, maybe without even realizing it. But what if that's the wrong goal?

What if we need to turn and go another way?

For more than fifteen years, I've been promoting the virtues of minimalism and owning less. I define *minimalism* as "the intentional promotion of the things we most value and the removal of everything that distracts us from it."[2] Minimalism looks different from one person to another, but it is something that everyone can benefit from.

To clear up a possible misunderstanding, this book is called *Uncluttered Faith* not because it is about believing less, as in abandoning unwanted doctrines or picking and choosing one's version of God. It is about intentionally uncluttering the physical possessions in our lives so that our faith can be uncluttered and unfettered, and we can reach our full potential through Christ.

In *Uncluttered Faith* I am making the case that my fellow Christians—*all* my brothers and sisters in Christ—need minimalism. Not because it is a trendy topic or because we're seeking self-actualization, but because it is God's design for our lives. In fact, simplifying our lives is one of the most widely overlooked keys for opening the door to the spiritual blessings God wants to give us—blessings like contentment, joy, spiritual growth, generosity, kingdom influence, and much more that we'll be considering in this book.

I'm not here to criticize you for your materialist tendencies.

Instead, I'm here to invite you to consider a better way. A life with *less stuff but more God*, as Amy Slenker-Smith put it. This could be one of the greatest turning points in your life!

Whether right now you are convinced, curious, or skeptical about minimalism, all I ask is that you keep reading and see not whether Joshua Becker is right but whether living the simple life is what Jesus Christ and the Holy Spirit are inviting us to. I think you'll discover that letting go of excess is essential to living faithfully and fully blessed—and it's a truth hidden in plain sight all throughout the New Testament, if we have eyes to see it.

My First Minimalism Epiphany

May I briefly introduce myself to you? Not that my own process of finding an uncluttered faith represents the only way to do it, but I'll be sharing my story (and those of many others I've met on their minimalism journeys) throughout this book, so you might as well start getting to know me now.

I am the oldest of three kids born to Roy and Patty Becker in Aberdeen, South Dakota. I am grateful to have been raised in a Christian family—in fact, all four of my grandparents loved and served the Lord. One of my grandfathers, Harold Salem, was a Baptist minister in South Dakota for seventy-eight years, working full time in the ministry until his death at the age of ninety-nine. Alongside my brother, I accepted Jesus into my heart at the age of five, walking forward during the final hymn following a Sunday evening service at First Baptist Church in Aberdeen.

Later, as a junior studying banking and finance at the University of Nebraska Omaha, I felt God's call to be a pastor. For the next fifteen years, I served as a pastor of student ministries at churches in Nebraska, Wisconsin, and Vermont and as associate pastor at a church plant in Arizona. My wonderful wife, Kim, whom I met in high school, has been an invaluable partner in ministry with me throughout it all. We cherish our two kids, Salem and Alexa.

One of the greatest turning points in our lives happened in 2008, while I was serving students at Essex Alliance Church in New England. If you've read my previous books or heard me speak, you may already know this first part of my journey. But if you're not familiar with my story, you need to understand how my life changed on that sunny Memorial Day weekend.

On that Saturday, I decided to clean our family's garage. All morning I hauled out dusty boxes, kids' playthings, gardening tools, and all kinds of other odds and ends and junk. As I ground my way through the work, I kept an eye on my then-five-year-old son, Salem, playing alone in the backyard because his dad didn't have time for him just then.

After a lunch break, I noticed our next-door neighbor June in her own yard, planting flowers and watering her garden. I waved to her and got on with my tasks.

By this point, I was trying to clean and organize all the stuff I had dragged out of the garage in the morning. It was taking much longer than I had expected. As I kept going, I thought about all the times lately when I'd felt discontented while taking care of our stuff.

Several hours into her own work, June said to me sarcastically, "Ah, the joys of homeownership."

Not knowing exactly how to respond, I replied, "Well, you know what they say—the more stuff you own, the more your stuff owns you" (something I'd probably read on a bumper sticker somewhere, without ever considering what it fully meant).

"Yeah," she said, "that's why my daughter is a minimalist. She keeps telling me I don't need to own all this stuff."

There it was! The insight I didn't know I'd been looking for and a more life-changing revelation than I could have imagined: *I don't need to own all this stuff.*

First, I looked at the pile of dirty, dusty possessions in my driveway. Second, I looked at my young son in the background, swinging alone on the swing set, and the full implications came into focus. *Not only are my possessions not bringing happiness into my life, even worse, they are distracting me from the things that do!*

In other words, I had the same realization that Amy Slenker-Smith had in the rainy parking lot of a Target.

My life would never be the same.

In my writing, speeches, and some personal conversations, I've told people about this insight many times. But what I've never shared before in print is that I would soon have another—more important and more life-changing—insight related to minimalism. One that ultimately formed the foundation for this book.

My Second Minimalism Epiphany

That Memorial Day weekend in 2008, the Becker family's minimalism journey began. Our decluttering went on for months. We eventually removed about two-thirds of our possessions, and with everything we discarded, life got a little easier. I was loving it! I was noticing practical, life-giving benefits with every load of items we removed.

At one point, while Kim and I were minimizing things in a bathroom, I turned to her and said, "Where has this been my entire life? How come no one told us about minimalism before? How come no one ever said, 'Hey, just own less. It's a better way to live life'?"

And that's when I had my second minimalism epiphany. See, it suddenly occurred to me that minimalism actually *wasn't* a new idea that nobody had told me about. My neighbor June wasn't the first person to say, "You don't need to own all this stuff." Jesus was promoting minimalism two thousand years ago! In fact, some of the most important words Jesus ever spoke dealt specifically with reining in riches and material possessions:

- "Go, sell your possessions and give to the poor, and you will have treasure in heaven. Then come, follow me" (Matthew 19:21).
- "Life does not consist in an abundance of possessions" (Luke 12:15).
- "Do not store up for yourselves treasures on earth" (Matthew 6:19).
- "Those of you who do not give up everything you have cannot be my disciples" (Luke 14:33).
- "What good is it for someone to gain the whole world, yet forfeit their soul?" (Mark 8:36).
- "You cannot serve God and wealth" (Matthew 6:24, NASB).
- "It is easier for a camel to go through the eye of a needle than for someone who is rich to enter the kingdom of God" (Mark 10:25).
- "Woe to you who are rich, for you have already received your comfort" (Luke 6:24).
- "Do not take a purse or bag or sandals" (Luke 10:4).

We'll be looking at such sayings from the New Testament throughout the course of this book. I think you'll be amazed at how using a minimalism lens will focus Scripture for you in a new way, making you say, "I never noticed that before" or "This finally makes sense to me." I've heard those reactions from countless people with whom I've spoken about these Scripture passages.

And by the way, when I use the word *minimalism* in this book, I'm not talking about a set of rigid rules that every person and every family must follow exactly. Nor am I talking about owning less just for the sake of it. I'm talking about working to align our lives fully with the teachings of Jesus on money and possessions. I believe you'll see what I mean as you the read the chapters ahead.

We don't have to be Bible scholars to recognize that Jesus called us to a life of simplicity and generosity over and over again. We just have to open our eyes to this theme when we're reading the Gospels.

But until my second epiphany, I had never done this before. Why not? Maybe it was because I didn't *want* to.

The Positive Side of Minimalism

The longer I thought about it, the more I realized that it wasn't only Jesus who had been trying to put me on the path to minimalism. Looking back over the course of my life, I could see that a number of people had made the same argument, just in different ways.

My parents modeled living within one's means and finding joy in simple tastes.

Financial advisers counseled me about having a budget, avoiding impulse buys, saving, and spending less than I made.

Pastors and mentors promoted generosity and warned me

against materialism and its negative influence on my spiritual health.

Environmentalists warned me against consumption and disposal and its impact on the environment.

Indeed, many people introduced me to the idea of living with less, even from a young age. But I began to realize that they had warned me about the evils of materialism, not invited me to experience the benefits of intentionally owning less. And there is a big difference—which explains why none of their warnings ever stuck.

Jesus, however, shows the positive side of minimalism in an incomparable way.

I want you to pay attention to what I'm about to say, because *this* is why the minimalism key so often goes unused, even though it's within reach of us all.

A lot of Jesus's commands to us are challenging: *Forgive those who have sinned against you. Take up your cross and follow Me. Pray for your enemies. Be a servant to all. Rejoice when you are persecuted. Deny yourself.*

None of these is easy or natural to do, but I think we all sense there is blessing on the other side of obedience in these areas. Repentance will give us a lightness of spirit. Forgiveness will let relational healing begin. Prayer leads to answers for us and others. And so on.

But I'm not sure we can so easily spot the benefits of living with less money and fewer possessions, at least not the benefits in this life. That kind of future here on earth looks like a picture of deprivation.

Or anyway, that's how I saw it.

The truth was, I didn't want to see Scripture's strong theme of Jesus calling us to give up possessions and luxuries. I tried to ignore it. Because when I read such things, I had a hard time seeing the personal benefit. Instead, I thought, *Jesus wants my life to be miserable. He wants me to give away everything to poor people, which I'm sure would benefit them, but that's going to leave me and my family living a boring life. I'll have to sacrifice a joyful life on earth. Maybe I'll have nice rewards in heaven, but I want to enjoy my life today. This is a trade-off I really would rather not make. Jesus can't mean what He's clearly saying.*

This was my attitude—until I actually started living out Jesus's teachings on money and possessions. As soon as I did, I began to understand on a deeper level that all God's greatest blessings lie on the other side of obedience. There is a better life for us in all His commands, *including* the ones to give away money and belongings.

Jesus's teachings on giving away our finances and possessions are meant not to make our lives miserable but to make them better, fuller, and more productive.

He created life. He knows the best way for us to live and make the most of our short time on earth. And He's saying to us, "Own less. You'll have more money, more time, and more freedom for the things that are most important to you and to Me—pursuits and passions that bring you more joy, more fulfillment, more meaning, and more life."

As we'll see again and again in the chapters ahead, many of the exhortations in God's Word become more understandable, and many subsequent promises become more attainable, when we remove the pursuit of money and possessions from our lives. Jesus knew how these things stand in the way of what God wants to do in and through us. My family and I have seen it. And thousands of Christian minimalists I've met in recent years have told me the same thing.

Uncluttered Faith won't lay out all the negative consequences or evils of materialism, although we can't help touching on some of them. Instead, chapter after chapter, this book will use commonly known Scripture passages to describe the spiritual blessings and abundant life available to us when we intentionally choose to own less stuff. I am going to lay out Jesus's promises for owning fewer possessions in a way I'd bet you've never seen.

Becoming Minimalist

The blog I began writing to record my experiences with minimalism—*Becoming Minimalist*—took off almost right away. That was a surprise! There was a lot of interest in simplifying, and people seemed to appreciate reading about my story and the practical things I was learning. The metrics on my readership grew exponentially. I began to believe that my website's growth was indicating a simple truth: Most people know deep down that they own too much stuff—and perhaps even feel emotionally weighed down by their excess belongings—and are looking for someone to validate their suspicion. Could that describe you too?

Because of the blog's expanding reach and its ever-increasing time demands on me, as much as I loved pastoring, I decided to transition gradually to full-time writing. First, while standing in the same garage where I'd had my original minimalism epiphany, I made the decision to take an associate pastor role at a new church in Arizona, which would allow me to spend more time on the blog and see where that went. For two years I worked two full-time jobs—in the church and on the blog—and then in October 2013, I resigned from my last church job to promote minimalism full time.

For more than fifteen years now, I've written blogs and books, given talks and guest sermons, taught decluttering courses, introduced an app, co-created two magazines, and provided professional training in the decluttering/organizing industry. This has given me the privilege of hearing from many thousands of people about their decluttering journeys. Not all are Christians of course, but many are. Among these Christian minimalists, the extent to which they have experienced a renewal of their faith as a consequence of minimizing has amazed me. I will be telling quite a few of their stories in this book. For now, I'd like to refer to just one of them: Kendra McDonnold.

Kendra is a mother to five boys in Lafayette, Louisiana. Several years ago, she found herself rushing through the house on a Sunday morning, scrambling to find a clean shirt, hoping her family would arrive at church on time.

"When I opened the closet, I just froze and my eyes began to well up with tears," she told me. "I don't know if it was the mounds of toys I had to step over that morning, the dishes in the sink, the hurried schedule, or the screams of protest from little ones in the next room. But in that moment I knew something needed to change. How could I be still and know that He was God when I was constantly rushing from one thing to another?"

That is when she began getting rid of what was no longer needed. "I removed the extra toys and clothes. I got rid of everything I could think of. I didn't want to do so many dishes, so I removed those as well."

The more she removed, the more margin she began to feel in her home.

As she recounted the story, she said something profound that I have found to be true in my own life as well: "I began to hear God's small whisper more frequently in my life. It's as if the more my physical environment quieted down, the better I could hear His voice in my life. Removing the material allowed for growth in the immaterial, and that is far more valuable to me now than anything I ever owned."

Wisdom from Fifty Years of Simplicity

Not only have I seen minimalism benefit countless people's spiritual lives, but I've seen the pursuit of owning less impact their friends' and neighbors' lives too. The spiritual blessings that minimalism unlocks aren't just ours but also reach to others. As a matter of fact, this book is directly related to one family's resolve to forgo consumeristic pursuits. Their decision from many years ago changed the trajectory of my life—and now has the potential to change the trajectory of yours.

Meet Dennis and Helen Dorenkamp.

When I was doing research for my last book, *Things That Matter*, I interviewed many people, including the Dorenkamps. This older couple lives down the street from me in Peoria, Arizona. With white hair and a broad smile, Dennis is kind, gracious, compassionate, and quick with a joke and contagious laughter. Helen is soft-spoken, loving, a perpetual encourager, and beautiful both inside and out.

Five decades ago, Dennis began his career selling insurance and quickly developed one of the most successful insurance agencies in his Minnesota town. But in his mid-thirties, with young children at home, Dennis felt called to become a pastor. So, he quit his job, even though this required him and his wife to live more simply on a much smaller income. His pastoral journey would take him from Washington to Minnesota and eventually to Arizona, where our paths would cross.

"As you look back on your life," I asked him, "what do you

think about your decision to give up an ever-increasing paycheck and financial success to pursue a life of serving others?"

His response came without hesitation. "If I had a hundred lives, I'd give them all to the ministry. There is nothing this world can offer that comes close to the richness of the blessings found in following God as closely as possible."

That's what minimizing our possessions and being intentional with our lives can do for us. It's not about what we give up. It's about the greater things we receive in return.

As a result of that phone call with Dennis—especially the joy with which he spoke of his decision—I spent five months seeking the Lord on the direction He would have me take with my life and work. I'd been a minimalism blogger for a long time by then, and I had received a lot of recognition for it. Accolades are nice. But as I wrote in *Things That Matter,* they can quickly become a distraction from the things that matter most.

While I ultimately opted to continue my work in writing about minimalism and the benefits of owning less, I did decide that fall to do more faith-based writing. I started an email newsletter and launched a website, Focus on Faith (https://focusonfaith.com), where I began publishing weekly devotional messages to keep hearts and minds focused on Jesus. I also started formulating my ideas for this book.

To me, this is not just another project. It is the culmination of my unique personal and professional journey. It is the book I believe God has called me to write. It represents an invitation to the Christian community to embrace a life of intentionality and deeper spiritual growth through owning less. This is a passionate subject for me, and I hope you'll absorb some of my passion as you read.

In the next chapter I'll tell you exactly why the message of *Uncluttered Faith* is so badly needed today.

2

The Culture We Are Swimming In

There's an adage that says, "A fish doesn't know it is wet." In other words, because a fish has never known life outside of water, it cannot conceive of any other way to live.

In the same way, most of us have never lived a life outside a consumeristic culture and society. Many historians date the rise of our modern consumeristic habits in America to the postwar 1940s.[1] Consumerism is all we have known, so recognizing it can be incredibly difficult.

But I'd like to try. Let me use some facts and statistics to paint a picture of how consumeristic we have become.

Consider first how our homes have grown. In 1949, the floor area of a new single-family home was 767 square feet, which amounted to about 224 square feet per person. By 2021, new houses had grown to 2,532 square feet on average—more than three times as large. Yet the average size of a household shrunk in those seventy-two years. So, today, the average floor area per person is 1,008 square feet.[2] Compared with our grandparents, today's generation of homebuyers have almost four times the house to pay for, furnish, heat, cool, clean, maintain, and worry about.

Is house-size inflation starting to seem like too much? For many, apparently so. Forty-two percent of Americans regret buying their homes because the maintenance and hidden costs are more expensive than they expected.[3] If you are a homeowner, there is a good chance you feel that weight every day.

Then there's all the stuff we put in our homes. One often-quoted estimate puts the total number of items in the average house at 300,000.[4] Even though we now live in homes with four times more square footage than that of our grandparents, 11 percent of households rent storage units to hold on to extra things.[5] And that number is growing astronomically; according to some studies, 38 percent of Americans have used or plan to use self-storage in the near future.[6] But that's not all: More than a third of Americans surveyed said their garages were so cluttered they could no longer park vehicles inside.[7]

If you wonder how owning that much stuff affects our daily lives, consider this: The average American spends two and a half days per year looking for items (such as TV remotes or car keys) that are lost in part because they got mixed in with all the house clutter. We spend more than $2.7 billion every year replacing lost items, and "more than half of us are *regularly* late for work or school due to frustrating searches."[8]

To get a sense of how consumeristic our culture has become, we don't even need to compare ourselves to our grandparents. We can look back just twenty-five years and see a huge difference. Americans buy an average of fifty-three new items of clothing each year, or about four times as many now as in the year 2000.[9] "On average—*average*—each piece will be worn seven times before getting tossed."[10] Can you guess how much of an American's wardrobe isn't worn *at all* over the course of an entire year? Correct answer: 82 percent.[11]

If you're starting to think this is just an American problem, let me stop you from heading too far down that road. This is a worldwide (or at least a developed-nation) issue. Belgians don't wear 88 percent of their wardrobe, Italians 81 percent, and Canadians 79 percent.[12] And Australia and New Zealand have larger average house sizes than the United States does.[13]

Do we need all the stuff we've got? Clearly not. Americans, on average, spend approximately $18,000 per year on nonessentials.[14] We love click-and-buy convenience, yet "74 percent of U.S. adults have experienced buyer's remorse after buying items online."[15] Half of Americans say they "feel overwhelmed by the amount of stuff in their homes"—a reasonable response when you realize that, collectively, we keep more than *five billion* unused items in our homes.[16]

If you think we've learned our lesson, you'd be wrong. Americans are not only continuing to collect stuff at unprecedented rates but also going into debt to do it. The U.S. credit card debt total keeps breaking records. In 2023, it crossed the threshold of $1 trillion.[17] That's *just* credit card debt. Taking all forms of debt into account, Americans owe about $18 trillion,[18] or a sum almost as large as the economy of China.[19]

An excessive desire for things is a perennial human temptation—witness the tenth commandment against covetousness. But a few global realities in recent years have brought consumerism to a crisis level.

One is the increase in both the affordability and accessibility of consumerist goods. There's nothing wrong with more efficient manufacturing and shipping—assuming workers aren't being exploited, of course. And there's nothing inherently wrong with companies like Amazon delivering products to your doorstep in a few hours with just the click of a button from your living room. But when goods become cheaper and easier to buy, without intentional consumer restraint, they become more ubiquitous as well.

Materialism's expanding influence may also be chalked up to our favorite phone addiction. In the words of one research report, "Social media, such as Instagram or Twitter, offer materialists new opportunities to pursue and satisfy their materialistic needs and goals. Preliminary work has already shown that materialists use social media to compare their possessions with those of other users and to accumulate digital possessions (in the form of friendships or followers)." In this way, social media contributes to higher levels of stress and lower levels of satisfaction with life.[20]

And then there's the disease we all wish we could forget. A 2022 study concluded, "The COVID-19 pandemic has led to an increase in the factors that typically facilitate the endorsement of materialistic values (e.g., higher media consumption, stress and anxiety, loneliness, death anxiety, and lower moods)."[21] We developed new habits of buying for comfort and security during COVID-19, and those habits haven't gone away.

Yet all these statistics are from the general population. What about Christians in particular? How materialistic are we?

Loving God *and* Gucci

A study published in the *Journal of Consumer Research* found only a slight correlation between professed Christian faith and lower levels of materialism.[22] It seems the habits of seeking wealth and possessions are ingrained nearly as much in Christians as in others.

Maybe you've observed this too: We Christians buy the same kinds of houses, wear the same kinds of clothes, distract ourselves with the same kinds of devices, and drive the same kinds of cars as anybody else. Our homes are just as full as everybody else's. We may be less materialistic than others to an extent (or at least I'd like to think so), but not so much that it's obvious.

Sociologist Peter Mundey argues in his book *Sacred Consumption* that consumerism is a "quasi-religion" itself. He says, "Consumerism is the 'something else' that motivates and guides . . . Americans when they recurrently shop for nonessentials—habitually upgrading and discarding in order to find contentment, fulfillment, and significance."[23] Mundey found that Christians in America both participate in and resist the religion of consumerism. To the extent we are participating in it, we are engaging in idolatry (Colossians 3:5). We preach against materialism, but we practice it just the same.

Of course, this is a problem not just in America but wherever Christians are enjoying affluence. One study of Christian teenagers in the South American nation of Chile and their attraction to luxury goods concluded, "Simply put, religious youth consumers love God, but they also love Gucci."[24] I think we all can relate to that tension.

Here's my point.

As Christians, we are swimming in a culture of materialism. But it feels so normal and expected, we don't realize we are drowning in it, sacrificing the fullness of life to it. We need to reassess our situation, grab on to a life buoy, and let it pull us to safety. That life buoy is minimalism—methodically and deliberately taking a different course with our money and possessions than the model presented by society.

When our minds are cleared of the fog of modern-day consumerism, we will find that choosing to intentionally own less isn't crazy; it's rational. What's crazy is the unending carnival of buying and accumulating we've all been participating in!

Maybe we would more readily choose simplicity if we had a clearer idea not only of how consumerism is deeply affecting us but also of what it is costing. I believe Jesus would say our excess of things is responsible for nothing less than choking off the Word of God in our lives.

Third-Soil Culture

According to New Testament scholars, the parable of the four soils (Luke 8:4–15) was one of the first that Jesus taught. It is also the first (and one of the few) that He takes time to explain to His disciples. So, it must contain truths He does not want us to miss.

The parable features a farmer who is sowing seed. The seeds fall on four kinds of soil, each of which offers a different reception for the seed. As Jesus explains, the soil types symbolize categories of people who hear the Word of God and respond differently.

If you are familiar with the story, you might remember that only the fourth soil produces a crop—a very bountiful harvest equaling "a hundred times more than was sown" (verse 8). The first three soils prove too inhospitable for the seed to bear fruit, but each for a distinct reason:

1. The seed that lands on the *hardened path* is immediately eaten by birds or trampled. This represents those who hear the Word of God but do nothing with it because Satan steals it away.

2. The seed that lands on the *rocky ground* sprouts but grows no roots. Jesus explains that this soil represents those who accept the Word with joy but fall away during times of testing or persecution because their growth is stunted.

3. The seed that lands among the *thorns* grows but is suffocated by the brambles. This soil represents those who hear and accept the Word, even growing roots, but fail to mature because their fruitfulness is choked out by the thorns.

Did you know that Jesus tells us exactly what thorns and weeds choke out the fruitfulness of God's Word in our lives? They are "life's worries, riches and pleasures" (verse 14).

Notice that He doesn't say the *love* of riches and pleasures strangles our fruitfulness. This is not just about our attitude toward wealth, although that is an important issue (1 Timothy 6:10). In some way, riches and pleasures themselves tend to keep us from being fruitful. As I'll explain later in the book, having money is not all bad, but it does come with spiritual risk.

If "life's worries, riches and pleasures" are threats to the fruitfulness of our lives for Christ, let's consider them more closely.

Life's worries. The context makes me think that Jesus is specifically referring to worries related to making money and getting all the things we want. Additionally, everything we already own burdens us with worry and stress. "Materialism is the mother of anxiety," Randy Alcorn writes.[25] Not a very loving mother is she? Our possessions take up physical space in our homes and mental space in our minds because they are something we are required to care for.

Riches. Another version of this parable refers to the "deceitfulness of wealth" (Mark 4:19). We work hard for our money, hoping it will bring us happiness and meaning, but the reality lets us down. So, we pursue still more money . . . which produces still more disappointment. We let ourselves be deceived over and over again about what money can do for us. Along the way, we neglect to consider its negative effects on us or how it distracts us from pursuing kingdom treasure.

Pleasures. We spend our money on things and experiences that we think will make us happy. And they probably do . . . for a little while. But too much focus on comfort and enjoyment leaves us empty inside. We begin to trust and look for solace and luxury in the worldly possessions we have acquired rather than the source of true life and fulfillment.

Consider the parable of the four soils with fresh eyes. Almost all the things our culture desires—wealth, possessions, luxury, comfort, and entertainment—are the very thorns that Jesus warned would keep us from being fruitful in the kingdom of God. The thorns of the third soil are not just planted in our whole society; they are promoted as good and lofty goals—even in Christian circles. And meanwhile, the crops God wants to sow in our lives are struggling.

The Great American Sin

For most of my life, I read that parable and thanked God that I was the fourth soil. Maybe I wasn't bearing a hundredfold crop for the Lord yet, but certainly I couldn't be described as any of the first three soils.

However, as my wife and I began removing the unnecessary possessions from our lives, we began to reassess the role of money, wealth, comfort, and society's influence in our hearts. (This is a crucial process of self-examination that I will be getting to in chapter 4.) And I started to understand that I wasn't the fourth soil.

I was the third soil.

And beyond that, I think the third soil describes the American church as a whole.

We have heard and accepted the Word of God. We are rooted. In fact, we have amazing resources and opportunities to grow in faith and deepen our roots everywhere we look. Yet are we reaching our full potential for bearing fruit? Certainly not. We have allowed life's worries, riches, and pleasures to choke out our fruitfulness.

The very pursuits most championed in our society are those that are keeping us Christians, both corporately and individually, from becoming all that God designed and desires us to be. And Jesus warned us against them two thousand years ago.

I'd go so far as to say that consumerism is *the* sin of the American church today. That is, it's our most characteristic, unrecognized, and deeply ingrained sin.

What other sin do we rarely criticize and in fact often celebrate? I certainly don't see us boasting about our sexual immorality or enslavement to intoxicating substances or drawing attention to our pride or hypocrisy. We'd never brag at a Bible study about how well our gossiping skills have developed, how impressive our lying has become, or how successful we've gotten at losing our temper. Those are the types of things we work hard to hide.

But we *do* flaunt our fashionable clothes and jewelry. We invite people over to show off the sizes of our new houses, and we post photos of our new cars on social media. We might "accidentally" let it slip how much we paid for the all-inclusive resorts on our last vacations or excitedly talk about the new drivers we bought for our golf bags. We refer to our extravagant purchases as "self-care." And we celebrate Black Friday and clearance-rack deals while we make lighthearted jokes about our shopping habits to our friends.

Meanwhile, we're focused on ourselves and our comfort and pleasure more than on honoring God and serving other people. Entangled by American materialism, we're spending more money on comfort and luxury for ourselves than on the basic needs of the poor and the expansion of God's kingdom.

It is my hope that we will begin to recognize how our physical possessions—both our accumulation and our pursuit of them—are hindering our fruitfulness as individuals and as the church. And that we will remove whatever is necessary so the full power of God's Spirit and kingdom can produce a harvest a hundred times greater than what was sown.

Another Way

We each serve the same God but in different ways—which means the way God will use the seed of His Word in our lives will vary. But when we remove the distractions, God's Word *always* produces a crop. The following examples show this to be true.

Robin Terrell from Waseca, Minnesota, discovered minimalism several years ago. She explained, "I just felt like life had become too hectic and there must be a different way to approach it. One evening, my curiosity got the best of me, and I decided to do an internet search on minimalism. I was immediately drawn to the idea of a calmer, more intentional life owning less."

She told me that she's not done with the process but has already seen a remarkable result. "With all of the progress that

I've made, I've had more time for daily devotions and prayer. I've also started keeping a yearly prayer calendar in which I offer to pray for people for a week during the year."

Once people found out about this, the prayer requests started pouring in. Some ask for a specific week; others share heartfelt needs they want covered in prayer. When their week arrives, Robin reaches out to let them know and asks whether they have any new requests.

What surprised her most was that many people without any faith background wanted to be included.

"People are desperate for God's love and intervention in their lives. Minimalism has freed me to both intercede on their behalf and become a living example of God's love for them. I never dreamed God would use me in this way. But I am honored and just want to be as faithful as I can."

Another story of minimalism paving the way for fruitfulness in the kingdom comes from Will and Tara Pierce of Springvale, Maine. Will is the pastor of a Baptist church, and Tara is his partner in ministry. Tara recently described to me how intentionally owning less has positively impacted their full-time ministry.

When they relocated to high-cost Maine from low-cost Kentucky, they moved into a 780-square-foot condo—far smaller than what most would expect for a growing family. They had two young children, a pastoral salary, and limited resources. Yet instead of wishing for more space, they embraced less.

The simplicity of their home became a gift. It meant less time spent cleaning. Lower expenses. Fewer distractions. And most important, more capacity to serve their church and community. Rather than being burdened by home maintenance or financial stress, they poured their energy into people. Their small home became a hub of hospitality, whether for a couple needing marriage encouragement, a church member grieving loss, or a group of teenagers simply needing a place to feel safe and seen.

"We invite people over all the time—from couples at the church to hosting teen nights," Tara told me. "People have poured into our home, and the only thing it is bursting with is joy and laughter."

She summed it up so well: "Minimalism has allowed us to love more, serve more, and give more."

Robin, Will, and Tara all have different roles in the kingdom, as do you and I. But we all serve the same God and desire for the same name of Jesus to be made known. Minimalism helps us recognize and overcome the pervasive culture of consumerism that keeps us from bearing abundant fruit in the greatest kingdom in the universe.

Becoming the Fourth Soil

There's something else to note about the third soil in Jesus' parable. The soil itself isn't necessarily bad. Just the opposite: It is fertile. But because the thorns and weeds have grown unchecked, the ground doesn't have room for a valuable crop to grow.

Yet what if a farmer comes along with a hoe and patiently and thoroughly chops out the unwanted plants? The fertile soil is then better prepared to receive the seed and bear a bountiful crop. It becomes the fourth soil.

This is exactly what we Christians who have given in to the third-soil culture can do in our lives: Chop out some misplaced passion here. Pull up the habit of incessant shopping at the roots. Toss away the unnecessary possessions that are keeping us from our God-given callings.

The biggest weeds grow in the most fertile soil, and so can the most fruitful plants. Our lives and faith hold so much potential. Unleash yours.

Become a minimalist, and the ground of your life will be ready for a whole new season of verdant, vibrant, abundant growth.

3

True Abundance

Emily McDermott started her minimalism journey in 2014, when she and her husband were amid fertility treatments. She says, "My eyes were opened to how decluttering my excess, simplifying my life, and saying no to what didn't serve me could help me make physical room in my home and emotional space in my heart to receive the baby we wanted so badly."

During this time, Emily's faith deepened. "I prayed more. I asked others to pray for me. The worship songs I sang were more meaningful. I saw myself in women in the Bible like Hannah, who desired a child so much and was so distraught that Eli the priest thought she was drunk.

"I also noticed the connection between the abundant life that Jesus called us to, the gratitude for what I had, and the generosity that flowed naturally as I let go of what I no longer needed. Abundance was no longer the amount of stuff I owned but having a full life with what mattered most to me."

Emily is now a mother of two and is experiencing firsthand the value of minimalism for a family. "I am so grateful for what minimalism continues to teach me so I can see God as my provider and be content with 'enough,' which has been recalibrated over the last decade as I acquire less, require less, and desire less."

We'll never find out what the *real* abundant life is if we try to live the false abundant life of ever more money, more stuff, and more frantic attempts to acquire the world. Those are just "life's worries, riches and pleasures," as the parable of the four soils says. Only minimalism can free us of the illusion so we can experience the genuine thing.

To the Full

I am going to rely on an important verse in John 10 to shape the conversation in this book. The verse is so significant that it has shaped much of my walk with Christ and the way I view His instruction and teaching.

In verse 10, Jesus says this: "The thief comes only to steal and kill and destroy; I have come that they may have life, and have it to the full."

In context, Jesus is comparing His offer of life to the world's. He speaks of the full and abundant life found only in Him and describes Himself as the gate through which that life can be accessed (verses 7, 9). But He doesn't start there. He begins the teaching by informing us of thieves (verses 1, 8)—those who come to steal and kill and destroy.

Yet He—the Good Shepherd, the Creator of the universe, and Lover of our souls—offers something new and better: life to the full. Blessings from God are better than anything this world can give. If this world were all we could attain, then we should try to accumulate as much of it as we could. But because a fuller, better, more abundant life is available through God, we should give up anything and everything necessary to take hold of it.

As missionary Jim Elliot said, "He is no fool who gives what he cannot keep to gain what he cannot lose."[1]

To fully appreciate and take hold of all that Christ provides, we must understand that Jesus does not just offer us eternity in heaven after death. He offers each of us a full and abundant life *today*—not necessarily an easy life but an abundant one. Life in the kingdom of God begins the moment we accept His gift of grace through faith.

Through God this life lived in the flesh can be marked by a living hope, a peace that passes understanding, and an inexpressible joy. And maybe even better than all that, we can live each day in relationship with and by the leading of the eternal, loving God of the universe. What a glorious gift! What amazing grace!

We have two choices: (1) the indescribable joy and blessing of life as we follow Christ or (2) the loss of life as we give in to the one who seeks to destroy us. Which option would you choose? Obviously, most of us would pick a life filled with the things of God rather than the things of this world.

If you need any further convincing that the pursuit of this world doesn't lead to happiness, would you be surprised to know that a slew of studies tell us the same thing?

Gangrene of the Soul

Proverbs 14:30 says, "A heart at peace gives life to the body, but envy rots the bones." And now science is confirming this truth from the Bible.

Numerous studies in the scientific literature today show the same thing—that worldly possessions do not provide nearly as much happiness as we think. In fact, many studies exist today that show how excess physical possessions actually harm our well-being.

The American Psychological Association recently published a paper showing that "the more highly people endorsed materialistic values, the more they experienced unpleasant emotions, depression and anxiety, the more they reported physical health problems, such as stomachaches and headaches, and the less they experienced pleasant emotions and felt satisfied with their lives."[2]

Research has accumulated over the years to support the adage that "money can't buy happiness." One review of twenty-three empirical studies concluded that "a consistent positive relationship was found between voluntary simplicity and well-being."[3]

On top of this, research has shown that highly materialistic individuals report lower levels of personal well-being, spanning across components such as lower life satisfaction, higher levels of depression and anxiety, and a lower sense of purpose in life. These trends appear to operate across income groups and regardless of a nation's GDP.[4]

In other words, there is a thief trying to steal life from us. And its name? Consumerism. Pursuing this world is never worth the price.

Leave a better legacy than a history of always pursuing more.

Eulogy for a Christ Follower

Although I'm no longer a paid church staff member, I still occasionally take on pastoral roles. Recently, I led a funeral for a fifty-year-old man who died suddenly. A tumor had been silently growing in his brain, unnoticed until he took a turn for the worse. In only three days, this man went from being a healthy, loving husband and father to lying in a coffin—his life seemingly taken in the blink of an eye.

He was highly successful in business, owning commercial real estate across the city and state. He spent thirty years building his business, but in the span of just seventy-two hours, none of that mattered anymore.

He was not a selfish, greedy man. Nor would I say he was unhealthily focused on growing an earthly empire. He followed Jesus and was gifted in business and with personality and magnetism.

I share this story because as I write these words trying to compare the kingdom of Jesus to that of this world, I am reminded of this man's life and his memorial service. You see, during that funeral, not one person stood up to share the address of a single building he owned or a business principle that marked his success. Instead, countless men and women, young and old, came forward to share about the impact he had on their lives. They talked about his love, his integrity, his passion for Christ, and his faithfulness to God.

People told of how the eternal destination of their souls was changed forever by his life and witness. And with each passing story, the pride on the faces of his family grew. His relationship with Christ was where lasting hope, peace, joy, and life were found. Through the lens of eternity, the kingdom of this earth shrinks in comparison to the greatness of God.

The abundant life—both now and for eternity—can be found in only one place: Jesus Christ.

Absolutely!

The world will seek to destroy our lives by tempting us with offers of shiny metal and plastic. The world and the father of lies will work every day to hijack our souls and hearts and redirect our passions away from God toward temporal things. But the world is a thief. And the abundant life is found only in Jesus.

How does the world steal and destroy life? By distracting us from the real thing.

In his book *Inner Excellence,* Jim Murphy explains that our pursuit of possessions isn't so much about the stuff itself; it's about looking for the abundant life in the wrong place. He writes it this way:

> Your greatest dream is not realized in having millions of dollars or perhaps a house overlooking the ocean. Your dream is *how you think these things will make you feel.* Perhaps those things will bring happiness as you imagine people complimenting you on your success, or will bring great experiences as you have your friends over to enjoy your waterfront home. But maybe they won't. Besides, money and material possessions aren't actually what you're *really* after.
>
> If you search your heart, beyond the desire for any measure of success, you'll discover, I believe, that what you really want is *to feel truly alive, filled with vitality, purpose and meaning—absolute fullness of life.*[5]

"Absolute fullness of life." Isn't this what we all desire to participate in with the one life we have to live? And isn't Jim right that even our pursuit of this world and its pleasures is an attempt to take hold of life at its fullest? Like a mouse lured into a trap, we fall for the counterfeit and miss the real and abundant life along the way.

It is interesting to me that Jesus offers us life "to the full" (John 10:10) but doesn't explain specifically what that means. Certainly, it includes eternity in heaven, but like I mentioned earlier, it is more than fullness of life after death. As the loving Creator of the world and life itself, no doubt God holds the keys for us to live our best lives today.

So, what does it look like to live a full life? Perhaps the best summary of what a full life consists of is found in Galatians 5:22–23. There, Paul describes exactly what we can expect when we truly follow Jesus and His Word: a life filled with "love, joy, peace, forbearance, kindness, goodness, faithfulness, gentleness and self-control."

As you read that list—the fruit of the Spirit—what quality do you *not* desire to be true of you? Love? Joy? Peace? Isn't everything on this list exactly how you want your life to be defined?

If you live from a place of love, joy, and peace, won't you consider that a full life? If your life is marked with faithfulness, gentleness, and self-control, won't you consider that success? If, at your funeral, men and women stand up to describe you as patient, kind, and good, won't that be enough? Don't these fruits describe the exact life you desire for yourself?

Maybe this is what life "to the full" means—a life godlier and more blessed than anything this world could ever offer.

The Becker Method: Get Started Now

Minimalism is not the only key to living an abundant life, but I've learned over the years that we can't truly live abundantly without it. You might taste some abundance, but you can't fully experience it while trying to live in both kingdoms. If you long for the full life Jesus offers but feel like something's holding you back, it might be the excess stuff you've grown used to carrying in your life and home. Physical possessions aren't just distractions from God's abundance; they're actually obstacles that keep us from it.

Of course, minimalism doesn't guarantee an abundant life in and of itself, but it clears a path for you to find that fullness. As you remove the clutter, you begin to uncover all that God has been extending to you all along. That's why I encourage you to start even now.

At the back of the book is the same seven-step Becker Method I teach to those who take my Uncluttered course. Even in this condensed form, the method descriptions should give you all the practical guidance you need. Turn there when you're ready to unclutter your home. To give you a preview, here are the steps:

Step 1: Find your motivation.
Step 2: Stay focused on the positives.
Step 3: Begin decluttering with a quick sweep.
Step 4: Declutter room by room, easiest to hardest, starting with lived-in areas.
Step 5: Notice and articulate the practical benefits of owning less.
Step 6: Establish clutter-free habits.
Step 7: Experiment with less.

As you unclutter your home, you will also be uncluttering your faith, because minimizing reveals spiritual benefits along the way. Each chapter to come focuses on one of the amazing benefits that opens for us when we own less and simplify. These are blessings that we may have experienced in part already but that we can never fully experience until we remove the distractions from our lives. I think that as you read about these blessings, you'll be thinking, *I want that!* over and over again.

As you minimize the possessions that represent the world's false offer of abundance, you will maximize your experience of the true abundance Christ freely gives.

4

Unmasking Your Heart's True Desires

When my wife and I began going through our home and removing possessions in 2008, we dropped off many piles of things at Goodwill and other local charities. Taking the first minivan load of unneeded things to the charities felt great. So did the second and third. We felt freer and lighter with each trip.

But by about the fourth load, we started to ask ourselves some difficult questions—namely, "Why in the world did we own four minivan loads' worth of things we didn't need? Why did we buy all this excess in the first place? What were we thinking?"

As difficult as this process was, eventually I began to understand that I was more in love with stuff than I ever realized: *I'm more susceptible to the world's messaging than I thought. Although I'd never admit it, maybe I'm trying to find happiness in the things I own, despite repeatedly saying I'm not. Maybe I've been comparing myself and trying to keep up with what others are buying. Maybe I've been trying to impress other people with the things I buy and the things I wear.*

Social-science researchers use a psychological assessment

tool called the Material Values Scale to measure an individual's level of materialism.[1] This scale is based on a series of statements that assess how much value the person places on material things across three key dimensions:

1. centrality (attaching great importance to acquiring possessions)
2. success (using possessions to signal achievement to others)
3. happiness (believing that possessions lead to life satisfaction)

We don't need to take a formal assessment to evaluate how deeply materialism is embedded not just in our culture but also in our personal value systems. In moments of peace and prayer, we can simply look inside our hearts to see what our past patterns reveal. Jeremiah 17:9 says, "The heart is deceitful above all things," so we'll find some things regarding money and possessions that aren't pretty. But that's okay. The point is, we need to understand ourselves better if we're going to open ourselves up to the abundant life Christ wants to give us.

I've found, in fact, that there are some things we simply cannot learn about ourselves until we minimize our possessions. Minimalism not only provides the space for self-discovery but also forces us to ask self-understanding questions, such as those my wife and I faced around our fourth minivan-load drop-off. In particular, minimalism helps us learn how attached we are to the world (always more than we think) and what sin or unhealthy desires in our hearts are motivating that.

To prove my point, let me show you something you may have never noticed in the Bible or thought about before. It occurs in the opening pages of the New Testament.

What Should We Do?

After four hundred years of prophetic silence in Israel, John the Baptist appeared. He was a prophet but more than that—the unique forerunner of the Messiah (Matthew 11:9–11). The Bible gives us a glimpse into how this great individual chose to live.

We forget that many of the New Testament people we look up to lived minimalist lives. And John the Baptist was the first of them all. "John's clothes were made of camel's hair, and he had a leather belt around his waist. His food was locusts and wild honey" (Matthew 3:4). He may have lived in a tent or cave in the wilderness, and clearly he didn't need clothes from Jerusalem's couturiers or gourmet restaurant food to eat. He seems to have been a crunchy, outdoorsy type of simple-living advocate.

This minimalist-prophet had a bold message for the crowds of his fellow Jews who came to him. "Do not begin to say to yourselves, 'We have Abraham as our father'" (Luke 3:8). John the Baptist's role in the kingdom was to prepare the way for Jesus, essentially announcing to the people that a new way to God was arriving. Relying on the name of their earthly father (Abraham) would no longer be enough. Change was coming, and it was time to get themselves ready for the Messiah.

As John's message began to break through, we find the people asking him specifically, "What should we do then?" (verse 10). If what John was saying about the Messiah was true, they wanted to know how to prepare themselves.

Think about it. This was John's big moment! His entire life and ministry had been leading up to this. He had been born to "prepare the way for the Lord" (verse 4), and here were the people, standing in front of him, as if to say, "Okay, we believe you. The Messiah is coming. What should we do to get ready?"

What would you have told the people to do had you been in John's place? If you were John the Baptist and the people of Israel had searched you out to ask how to prepare their hearts for the coming Messiah, what advice would you give them?

Maybe you would tell them to study the Old Testament prophecies so they would recognize Jesus when He fulfilled them.

Maybe you would tell them to spend time in worship or offer sacrifices in the temple so they could recognize God's voice.

Maybe you would encourage them to fast and pray. Or you would tell them to listen closely to the guy who is about to heal the sick and give sight to the blind.

But John does none of that! His answer to the specific question "What should we do then?" is truly remarkable and absolutely life-altering. We can't miss it.

Everything he told the people to do to get ready for Jesus focused on their money or physical possessions. Unbelievable! Take a look:

> To the crowds he said, "Anyone who has two shirts should share with the one who has none, and anyone who has food should do the same" (verse 11).
>
> To some tax collectors he said, "Don't collect any more than you are required to" (verse 13).
>
> To some soldiers he said, "Don't extort money and don't accuse people falsely—be content with your pay" (verse 14).

And that was the end of his instruction. In other words, his advice to the people—the one thing at the top of his mind when he thought about preparing hearts for Jesus—was this: "Get rid of the stuff you don't need, and be content with what you have."

Why was that John's response? Because he knew that we can never fully prepare our hearts for Jesus until we remove the world from our hearts. And we can never remove the world from our hearts until we discover what keeps us tied to it.

For me, this begs an interesting question: How does sharing our clothes and food with the needy, as well as resisting the temptation to take more than we deserve, prepare us for God's message?

Sure, giving clothes helps the poor stay warmer. Giving groceries feeds the hungry. Saying no to cheating and extortion protects the vulnerable. Doing the right thing in these areas helps others. I've always known that to be true, but why is it one of the most important steps we can take in our relationships with Jesus?

It's because the change process begins with eliminating the excess from our lives. For this, we need some moments of self-reflection that help us recognize when materialism is influencing us, and why.

Brother Issues

Little-known fact: I have a twin brother. We're fraternal, not identical, twins. If you'd see us next to each other, you wouldn't even know we were brothers. He's six foot four, has broad shoulders, and is bald. I'm six feet tall, with a slim frame, and well, if you know me at all, you know I have a full head of hair. We're so different physically, my mom likes to joke that there is probably another set of twins somewhere in the world who look just like us.

Jerrod is one of the finest Christian men I know. I love him and he loves me. Nevertheless, like most brothers, we've always been competitive. Unfortunately, through no fault of his, I've felt on the losing end for most of my life.

With his confident, outgoing personality, Jerrod was always more popular than I was. In school he was bigger, stronger, and more successful in sports. To put it into perspective, while Jerrod was a starting tight end on the varsity football team, I was playing tennis on the JV squad—and I quickly learned that varsity football players get invited to more parties than JV tennis players. He was on the homecoming court, and I was in the stands watching him.

It didn't end in high school. Jerrod went on to play basketball in college. Immediately after college, he took over a successful masonry business and outstripped me in terms of moneymaking. I've often felt inferior to or jealous of my brother, right along with all the love I have for him.

But it wasn't until I became a minimalist that I realized just how internally driven I was to keep up with him and how that influenced my decisions. So much of what I did was designed to impress Jerrod or to draw my parents' attention by creating a favorable contrast with my brother. I'm not proud of it, but this is the truth. Neither my parents nor my brother brought about any of this; I invented it in my heart.

The first Christmas after adopting minimalism, Kim and I were traveling back home to South Dakota to spend the holiday with my parents as well as my brother and sister and their families. By this time, I was wearing a simple "uniform" of mostly khaki pants and black V-necked T-shirts. I liked it—my closet was so much roomier, and choosing clothes in the morning took no time at all. Around the church office where I worked, I was even becoming known for my signature style—wearing the same thing every day is the quickest way to become iconic, after all.

But packing my suitcase for this trip felt different. In fact, while filling it with only khakis and now well-worn T-shirts, I began to feel insecure about my wardrobe for the holiday and what impression I would be making.

I stopped what I was doing to think about *why* I was feeling uneasy in this new circumstance.

This would be the first time my family of origin would see me in my new simplified apparel. I wouldn't be wearing any new clothing or trendy fashions. I wouldn't have a watch or jewelry other than my wedding band. I would be wearing nothing that sent an external sign of success.

Meanwhile, Jerrod would sport a variety of fashionable clothes, whether he was in casual wear or dressed up to go out. Compared to him, would I look like a loser? Should I consider making an exception to my new minimalist habits and go out and buy a few new things to wear on the trip?

I discovered two things about myself in that moment.

First, I still had some brother issues to work out.

Second, many of my spending habits and life decisions had been, and still were, motivated by a desire to impress people. It was a hard lesson to learn but an important one for my personal and spiritual development.

As a result of these insights, I came to a conclusion: I had to run out to the store right away and buy some new clothes. Just kidding.

Regardless of how my family would react to my new wardrobe, I didn't *want* to buy clothes I didn't actually need! I could be content, even happy, with my simple clothing. Christmas—the biggest season of material excess of the calendar year—might be the best possible time to stick to my minimalist style.

With a nod to myself, I went back to filling my suitcase.

Getting to the bottom of our motivations like this can help us undergo healing and sanctification in our approach to stuff. In my early stages of owning less, I began to understand that taking steps to remove the world from our lives *forces* us to wrestle with those questions in ways we might never experience otherwise.

John the Baptist's instructions in Luke 3 begin to make perfect sense once we actually live out what he says and start removing our excess possessions.

Seven Things You May Learn About Yourself

Your self-discovery through minimalism will be unique to you. But in my years of working with people to unclutter their homes, I've discovered some common motivations that tend to underlie our overaccumulation of possessions. As you're looking inward to find what has been driving you specifically, be open to discovering motivations such as these:

1. **You are looking for security in your possessions.**

   The logic goes like this: If owning some material possessions brings security (a roof, clothing, reliable transportation, and so on), owning excess will surely result in even more security. But after our most basic needs are met, the actual security we derive from things we own is much less stable than we believe. They all perish, spoil, or fade. And they can disappear faster than we realize.

2. **You think buying things will make you happy.**

   Nobody would ever admit they search for happiness in material possessions—we all just live like we do. We buy bigger houses, faster cars, cooler technology, and trendier fashions hoping we will become happier because of it. Unfortunately, the actual happiness derived from excess physical possessions is fleeting at best.

3. **You are more influenced by the world's advertising than you think.**

   It seems we are marketed to on every screen, billboard, and flat surface in the world today. And every advertisement carries the same message: "Your life will be better if you buy what we are selling." We hear this messaging so many times and from so many angles, we begin to subtly believe it. But when we peek behind the curtain, we realize it's all smoke and mirrors. This is not a complete condemnation of the marketing industry; it is simply a call to realize their messaging affects us more than we realize.

4. **You use your possessions to try to impress other people.**

   In a wealthy society, envy quickly becomes a driving force for economic activity. Once all our basic needs have been met, consumption must be based on something more than needs. It becomes an opportunity to display our wealth, importance, and financial success with the world. Sometimes it's very personal, as with me and my brother; at other times, we'd just like to impress anybody.

5. **You are motivated by jealousy and comparison.**

   Comparison seems to be a natural state of our humanity—we notice what other people are buying, wearing, and driving. Our society encourages these comparisons. And all too often we buy stuff we don't need just because people in our friendship circles have done the same. A culture fixated on praising excess will always misdefine true success.

6. **You use physical things to mask your weaknesses and insecurities.**

   We mistakenly look for confidence in the clothes we wear or the cars we drive. We seek to recover from loss, loneliness, or heartache by purchasing unnecessary items. We seek fulfillment in material things. And we try to impress others with the things we own rather than with the people we are. But these pursuits will never fully satisfy our deficiencies. Most of the time, they just keep us from ever addressing them.

7. **You are more selfish than you'd care to admit.**

   It can be difficult to admit that the human spirit is hardwired toward selfishness and greed, but both the Bible and history make a strong case for this. We seek to grow our personal kingdoms by accumulating more and more things. This has been accomplished throughout history by force, coercion, dishonesty, and warfare. Unfortunately, selfishness continues to surface in our world and our lives even today.

The seven motives above do not constitute an exhaustive list. I could brainstorm a few more unworthy motivations for ownership, and so could you. For instance, *We tie our identities to what we own; we buy to feel in control;* and *we buy out of boredom or lack of purpose.* None of these make us feel too good about ourselves, do they?

To be honest, I don't think there is *any* godly rationale for owning more stuff than we need. *All* our motivations for doing so are unworthy.

So, I hope that as we dig down into our motivations for greed and materialism, we will more clearly see not just the emptiness of this approach to life but also the heart issues we need to deal with to overcome it . . . and then to make a permanent break from the kingdom of money and possessions to the kingdom of God. This is how we prepare our hearts to meet and grow closer to Jesus.

A Transformative Season

Laura Morgan lives in Green Mountain Falls, Colorado. She discovered minimalism during a challenging season of life after her son was born and while her marriage was in crisis. She says, "The act of letting go of physical possessions has mirrored my emotional and spiritual journey. I've had to sift through and declutter thoughts and beliefs that no longer served me. I uncovered lies—mental clutter—that hindered my spiritual growth and kept me from embodying love and Christlike qualities."

Despite the pain she experienced, these years and this process of minimizing her possessions have pushed Laura to reflect deeply on what she truly believes and why. "When I stripped everything down to what truly matters," she says, "I found it was all about relationship—loving God and being loved by Him, loving others and being loved by others. I want to live my life casting off anything that hinders me from this calling. The past few years have been a transformative season for me both inside and out."

She summarized the change in her life this way: "This became about so much more than decluttering; it helped guide me into a process of sanctification and becoming more like Christ."

Just like Laura, me, and countless others, as you simplify your life, you'll find it easier to reflect honestly on your relationship to money and things. The things you see may not be what you were hoping to, but don't turn away from them. Learn from them. And change.

Today, in some way, God is drawing you toward a better, more meaningful lifestyle—the one He dreamed for you when He created you. Having a simpler lifestyle will make it easier for you to learn about that too.

5

Closer to Jesus

My friend Glen Van Peski has more diverse and unusual interests than almost anyone else I know. He is best known for helping "revolutionize backpacking by creating ultralight equipment" through his company, Gossamer Gear, "which allows people to take less so they can do more in the wilderness."[1] He heads into some of the most rugged and beautiful wilderness in the world for days, carrying only six pounds of gear on his back. And he frequently hosts trips for journalists, business executives, Hollywood celebrities, and others, introducing them to the joy of going farther in nature while carrying less.

Why take so little while backpacking? Glen says, "People pack too much in their packs based on their fears, on what might happen, and what they might need to deal with it. Then, once they have a heavy pack, that pack comes between them and their best trip. The extra weight means they can't explore as far and they don't enjoy as much as they would without the weight."[2]

Glen is a bold Jesus follower, and the spiritual implications of his insights about ultralight backpacking are not lost on him. "I wonder," he says, "if sometimes our collecting 'stuff' isn't trying to fill a void that we really need God for."

One of the most revolutionary lessons Glen has learned while hiking tens of thousands of miles throughout his lifetime is that the possessions we go through life with sometimes keep us from going both fast and far. He is adamant about the backpack weight of those he accompanies on their journeys, because if one member of the group tries to bring too much, they will inevitably hold back the rest of the group. And like hikers, the less we own, the easier we can travel through life. Glen sums it up this way: "The philosophy that guided my ultralight backpacking innovations—'take less, do more'—also guided me in just about every aspect of my life."[3]

Glen's philosophy reminds me of another leader.

Jesus spent a lot of His ministry years traveling light around Israel with His disciples. He's with us on our journeys too. He's our companion, our leader, our pacesetter. Jesus leads us not on hikes to beautiful waterfalls or mountain summits but to something even greater: the truly abundant life. It should be our goal to stick as close to Him as possible, regardless of what we have to leave behind.

Let's eagerly remove all that weighs us down so we can travel faster and farther—and closer to Jesus—than we ever imagined.

Letting Go of the Weight

Years ago, in my early days of minimalism, my sister-in-law Dodie asked me a question I wasn't sure how to answer: "Do you think it is a sin to buy things we don't need?"

Around the same time, I was beginning to see the spiritual connections between living a simple life and being faithful to

Jesus, and I was reading Jesus's teachings on money and possessions in a brand-new way. But would it be accurate to categorize overbuying as a *sin*? If so, then most of us (me included) have done more sinning than we know and are currently engaged in this kind of sin to an extent we'd hate to admit. The evidence is all around us in our homes.

I finally responded to Dodie, "There is no doubt that in some circumstances it is sinful to waste our financial resources buying the things of this world that contribute to our excess. But not every hindrance to the Christian life is a sin."

In making this distinction, I had in mind Hebrews 12:1–2, where the metaphor isn't hiking (Glen Van Peski's favorite) but the related sport of running: "Since we are surrounded by such a great cloud of witnesses, let us throw off everything that hinders and the sin that so easily entangles. And let us run with perseverance the race marked out for us, fixing our eyes on Jesus, the pioneer and perfecter of faith."

Notice that here we are called to remove two things from our lives: (1) "everything that hinders" and (2) "the sin that so easily entangles." It seems the author of Hebrews differentiated between things that hinder our walk and actual sin. Some things may not reach the level of sin, yet still be unwise encumbrances for running the Christian race.

This may seem like a small point, but it is incredibly important to understand. The Holy Spirit—the ultimate Source of all Scripture, including this passage—goes beyond telling us to remove sin from our lives to follow Christ as best we can. He advises us to throw off *anything* and *everything* that might hinder us from fully following Christ with our energy and attention.

With Jesus as our leader and goal, we want to go beyond just eliminating sin to taking every possible measure so we can follow Him as best we can.

Watching television may not be a sin, but if it keeps us from running our best race, it is a hindrance that should be thrown off. The same may be said of other forms of entertainment as well as hobbies, leisure, travel, and the trivial—the kinds of things that could cross the line from being harmless activities if they cause us to take our eyes off Jesus.

Let me ask you a bold question: Is it possible our overaccumulation of possessions has become a hindrance to our following Christ? Surely it is so. An overabundance of possessions is clearly an encumbrance that holds us back. It's literally bulky, weighty, and space consuming. It demands our attention and consumes our resources. All that stuff we own and have to take care of can *absolutely* slow us down in our devotion and mission for Jesus.

Is it a sin to overaccumulate physical possessions? In some circumstances, probably.

Is it a hindrance to our walk with Christ? In almost every circumstance, absolutely.

Free Joshua

I can attest that minimalism has helped me follow Jesus better by removing the weight of caring for possessions. Let me mention just three of the many areas where it has given me freedom.

My time

I chuckle to myself when someone says or messages to me, "I know you're really busy, but it would be great if we could get together." I don't know whether they say that because it just sounds nice, because it's culturally the thing to say, or because they really think I accomplish a lot and therefore must be hard-pressed for time. But I chuckle because, honestly, I'm not that busy!

As a result of the simplicity of my home and business, I've got plenty of time to meet with friends who want to hang out or other folks who want to talk with me because they're going through a hard time. I've got time to stay involved in the lives of my wife and kids. I've got time to lead a small group at our church, volunteer every Sunday morning, attend church each week, and still be available to offer some formal pastoral services (funerals and weddings) when needed. I've got time for prayer and meditation, for daily exercise, or for getting out and refreshing myself in nature. All that and, to be honest, I probably still waste more time each day than I should!

My space

While perhaps not as often considered as the availability of time, the availability of *space* can also be a valuable benefit of decluttering.

One time, for example, a former member of my youth group in Vermont died suddenly while in Phoenix, where I now live. It was shocking and tragic, and as sad as it was for me, I knew it would be much harder on his family back East. When I called his father to express my sympathy, I asked, "Is there anything I can do to help?"

The grieving dad said, "Actually, yes. We need someone local to pick up and store his truck until we can get down there to drive it home."

My garage wasn't cluttered with tools or boxes or overflow stuff from the house. A car bay was already free. So, I told the dad, "No problem."

The truck sat in my garage for several weeks. I was able to

help in that small but crucial way because we had minimized our garage.

And we have been able to use the available space in our home in numerous other ways throughout the years: keeping supplies for The Hope Effect, storing the contents of our neighbors' home when they moved, providing a temporary space for a friend's office furniture when he was unexpectedly forced to relocate, and providing a place to stay for visitors. We're happy that we can serve God and be hospitable in these ways because our home has space available.

My finances

We used to be like most Christians, wishing we could give more money to church and charity but not feeling like we could afford it because of all that we were already spending our money on for ourselves.

By lowering our costs for possessions, we can now give much more than we used to. We tithe to our church and provide ongoing support for our nonprofit, The Hope Effect. In addition, we have the freedom and opportunity to give to other mission and relief projects and causes we believe in, including several current church plants here in the Phoenix area.

Having money in reserve to contribute when a need suddenly comes up in someone else's life is a luxury one can never buy at a store.

Financial freedom based in minimalism is a benefit that goes on year after year. And even though we're not notably wealthy, contemplating the cumulative amount we have been able to give over the years gives me a lot of satisfaction.

Ready to Answer the Call

"We never would have been able to follow God so closely if we had been bogged down by debt and possessions." Jennifer's comment to me immediately caught my attention and drew me into her story. I asked her to share more.

It started with heavy spring rains. The finished basement of Jennifer and Matt Polsdofer's house in Forest City, Iowa, flooded, damaging a lot of the stuff they stored there and requiring them to move everything else out of the basement or pile it in the middle of the room. "The kicker," she told me, "is that we didn't even want the stuff! It just lived in our basement, and now we had to move it all." This became an almost annual routine, until one year it made them think, *If we weren't holding on to all this stuff in the first place, we wouldn't have to go through all this!*

They went online and started devouring articles at Becoming Minimalist and other sites related to minimalism and simplicity, then began purging. With fewer things cluttering the house, life got easier.

But the real benefit of their minimizing appeared later.

After a couple of years, Matt felt the call to become a full-time pastor. He applied to seminary and was enrolled in a program with free tuition and a living stipend. Having already weeded out their possessions years earlier, they now found it relatively easy to sell the rest of their belongings. They moved across the country in their minivan so he could complete his internship. This wouldn't have been possible if they weren't minimalists.

The family is continuing the minimalist lifestyle and seeing new benefits today. "Now that we have four kids," says Jennifer, "minimalism is a daily lifesaver. Our house is chaotic enough, but I can't imagine what it would look like if we lived like most American families."

Lacking One Thing

To take the discussion up a notch, let me ask you this: What if your possessions are not just keeping you from walking closer with Jesus; what if they are preventing you from experiencing the quality of life He wants you to have? If you knew that to be true, how much of your stuff would you get rid of?

Let's consider another story from the New Testament.

One day a young man who possessed much wealth, many goods, and thus a high social status came up to Jesus with an important question. We don't know his name, but he has historically been referred to as the rich young ruler. He asked Jesus, "Good teacher, what must I do to inherit eternal life?" (Luke 18:18).

We often equate eternal life with getting into heaven when we die. But Jesus described it as something more than that. He understood it as a reality that can be participated in today. In a prayer to His Father, Jesus defined it specifically: "Now this is eternal life: that they know you, the only true God, and Jesus Christ, whom you have sent" (John 17:3).

Keeping that definition in mind, let's consider Jesus's answer to the rich young ruler about how he could receive eternal life.

After He listed some of the commandments and the rich young ruler claimed to follow them, Jesus told him, "You still lack one thing. Sell everything you have and give to the poor, and you will have treasure in heaven. Then come, follow me" (Luke 18:22).

Now, I've heard this story taught many times from many different teachers. And almost every single time, the pastor will say, "I know Jesus said, 'Sell your possessions and come follow Me.' But Jesus didn't mean it literally. What He really meant was 'Whatever is keeping you from following Me, you need to get rid of it.'"

And everybody in the room will think of the one sin that continually trips them up and will nod their head in agreement that they should remove it from their life. Likewise, everyone quietly breathes a sigh of relief that they don't actually have to sell their possessions to fully experience eternal life. As if the things we've accumulated—our bank accounts and all the worldly objects we manage and store every day—*aren't* keeping us from fully following Jesus and experiencing Him fully in our lives! After all, you can't take up your cross if your hands are full of worldly possessions, although we sure do try.

So, let me ask you—what if Jesus actually meant what He said? If Jesus told you that to fully know Him and the Father and to inherit full, eternal life today, you needed to sell all the unnecessary possessions in your life, could you do it?

The rich young ruler felt he could not. My grandfather used to describe Luke 18:23 as one of the most melancholic verses in all the Bible. It says, "When he heard this, he became very sad, because he was very wealthy." The young man left grieving and distressed. In other words, he would rather keep his stuff than fully experience following Jesus.

Take a moment and allow God to rest that truth on your heart for a moment. The young man would rather keep his possessions than give it all up in pursuit of Christ.

Jesus's words were so weighty, so countercultural, that even His disciples wanted to make sure they heard Him correctly. "Who then can be saved?" they asked (verse 26).

If we don't read about the rich young ruler and walk away

asking, "Who then can be saved?" we're completely missing the importance of the story.

Randy Alcorn, author of *Money, Possessions, and Eternity*, brings this story into the present, commenting on the disciples' response: "This statement left the disciples 'greatly astonished' (Matthew 19:23–25). They did not understand the barrier that wealth presents to genuine spiritual birth and growth. Apparently, neither do we."[4]

Spiritual formation teacher Richard Foster goes even further. He suggests that Jesus's instruction to the rich young ruler might be more applicable to us than to him. "If, in a comparatively simple society, our Lord lays such strong emphasis upon the spiritual dangers of wealth, how much more should we who live in a highly affluent culture take seriously the economic question?"[5]

I believe Jesus meant exactly what He said—that it is impossible to grab hold of Him while clenching tightly to the world. On the other hand, when we remove our possessions, we can follow Him more closely. And the result of that is treasure in heaven, not treasures here on earth. That is a trade we would all be wise to make!

The Camel and the Needle

With the rich young ruler standing there, dejected and melancholy, Jesus looked at him and communicated a warning. His admonishment is frankly startling, and I believe it is not just for the young man or the disciples listening in but for all of us: "How hard it is for the rich to enter the kingdom of God! Indeed, it is easier for a camel to go through the eye of a needle than for someone who is rich to enter the kingdom of God" (Luke 18:24–25).

This warning may be as important to us as any in the New Testament, but rarely do we meditate on what it means in our lives.

It is next to impossible for a rich person to enter the kingdom of God.

One reason we tend to ignore the significance of this statement is that most of us don't think we are rich. We're just middle class, about the same as most people in terms of our wealth and possessions. We believe Jesus's warning is important for other people to think about, but not us.

Yet in reality, almost everyone reading this chapter *is* among the rich. According to one online calculator, if you make $50,000 per year, your income puts you in the top 2 percent worldwide for income. Even an annual income of $20,000 puts you in the top 10 percent.[6] (These numbers vary slightly based on household size, but the point remains.)

We live in a world where half the global population lives on less than seven dollars per day.[7] That is lower than the *hourly* minimum wage in every state in America.

We *are* rich. And when Jesus said it is easier for a camel to go through the eye of a needle than for us to enter the kingdom of God, we should probably pay attention. What is it about *our* wealth and *our* possessions that might be keeping us from experiencing kingdom living today?

But there's another reason we may read this warning from Jesus and think it doesn't apply to us. We may say to ourselves, *I have put my faith in Jesus and am saved by His grace. I know I am going to heaven. So, this verse must be directed at rich people who have not accepted Him.*

However, living squarely in the kingdom of God today and getting into heaven after the final judgment are two different things. We can be saved but still miss out on the calling and blessing of living in the kingdom today if we resist God's will in our lives.

For those with earthly wealth, learning to live in the center of God's will today requires humility, which is not easy. It requires intention each day to pull our gazes off the things of this world and to focus on Christ. It requires us to identify and overcome the deception of riches. And it requires us to use our money to no longer gather earthly treasures but to store up heavenly ones.

Pack Light

Why does Glen Van Peski require his fellow hikers to pack light? Because there is so much beauty to experience in the world. And the lighter we pack, the more we can see, the more we can experience, and the more we can be changed through the experience—not to mention the more stories we have to tell about the trip.

The same is true for our faith. When we intentionally own less, something incredible happens: We create space to hear God's voice more clearly and free our lives to step boldly into the future He desires for us. The noise of consumer culture fades, and the voice of the Holy Spirit grows louder. And even better, a hindrance is removed so that we can run the race faster, longer, and with greater perseverance.

This is the offer of Christ's command to "sell your possessions and come follow Me"—eternal life today and treasures in heaven in the future.

The less we carry, the more we gain.

6

A Life Without Greed

When I was a youth pastor in Menomonie, Wisconsin, I had the privilege of getting to know a church member named Donna. Tall with long, dark hair, she was a wife, the mother of two, and a pediatric nurse at a local hospital.

One night Donna helped deliver a baby girl who was born with severe special needs. Upon learning about the baby's needs, the birth mother immediately abandoned her at the hospital.

The next day, Donna said to her husband, "I'm not sure what to think, but I believe God is calling us to care for this baby girl."

They prayed about it, consulted with their son and daughter and closest friends, and soon after adopted the newborn. They knew raising this girl with special needs wouldn't be easy, but they wanted to be faithful to God and knew they could provide a loving home for her.

Only six months later, Donna's husband died suddenly.

So there was Donna, alone, grieving a lost husband and trying to raise three children, including a newborn who required almost every ounce of her attention.

As their youth pastor, I provided what support I could to the older kids, Caitlin and Sam. I also got to know Donna and the younger daughter, Jamie. I saw firsthand how tough things could get for them. And I saw the faith and hope Donna radiated despite their daily challenges.

Many years have passed, and I've kept in touch with this family. Caitlin is now married and has a daughter of her own. Sam has started a career. Meanwhile, Donna still provides care for Jamie seven days a week. The home she shares with her daughter is quite modest, as you would expect with someone who has been living on a curtailed income for years. She doesn't wear fancy clothes, drive a nice car, or travel to exotic locations. She gets by with help from friends and family members.

To many people looking in from the outside, Donna wouldn't look externally successful. But do you know what I see when I look at her?

Donna looks like Jesus to me.

She has lived a life of love and service to the least of these—just like Jesus. She may not have many earthly possessions to show for it—just like Jesus. But her first desire, for as long as I've known her, has been for the kingdom of God and the people He loves—again, just like Jesus.

What do *we* really value in life? When we get down to it and search our hearts, is our greatest goal to live lives of ease, comfort, and entertainment for ourselves or of love, service, and faithfulness to God who created us? Would you rather live a life wrapped up in self or patterned on the One who came to serve rather than to be served?

Owning less requires us to both confront and overcome greed in our lives to be successful on the journey. We know greed doesn't really make us happy, and social science has proved it.[1] It is not a trait any of us would like used to describe our lifestyles.

If we really want to model our lives after the life of Jesus, we need to confront the motivations that keep us from that. In Luke 12, we'll discover two of them—one we'll get to in this chapter and one in the next. And we'll also discover how rethinking the physical possessions we accumulate both reveals those motivations *and* provides the beautiful pathway out of them.

Jesus, Minimalist

As we saw in chapter 4, John the Baptist was a minimalist. So was Jesus.

Jesus went so far as to choose a homeless, wandering existence for the period of His ministry. He pointed it out Himself: "Foxes have dens and birds have nests, but the Son of Man has no place to lay his head" (Luke 9:58).

That's something to remember when we're tempted to speak glibly about being Christlike. We *say* we want to live like Christ, but do we really want what that might look like? We desire certain spiritual qualities to be true of us—but are we willing to give *all* that it takes to make that a reality in our lives? It is easy to overlook what Christlikeness might mean for our homes, bank accounts, and possessions when the world doesn't normalize that kind of life and even argues against it.

Jesus had something to say about the type of attitude it would take to seek Him first. And wouldn't you know it, His teaching was entirely centered (yet again!) on possessions and money.

Let me set the scene for you. One day someone in a crowd called out to Jesus, "Teacher, tell my brother to divide the inheritance with me" (Luke 12:13).

Such a demand is not hard to imagine, is it? Many of us know or have been part of families who were torn apart over disagreements about inheritance. Sadly, the passing of wealth from one generation to the next can often cause our human tendency toward greed to erupt from below the surface.

Jesus would not let Himself get roped into the ugly family dispute like the man wanted. He wasn't in a place to pronounce any binding judgment on the parties anyway. Instead, Jesus turned the interruption into a life-giving teaching opportunity for everyone within listening range.

"Watch out!" He told the crowd. "Be on your guard against all kinds of greed; life does not consist in an abundance of possessions" (verse 15).

Let's read that again but more slowly: "Be on your guard against all kinds of greed." For "life does not consist in an abundance of possessions."

I am going to propose that this warning may be even more relevant to us today than it was to those in the crowd listening to Jesus. Most of us would nod our heads in agreement but then turn around and live as if the warning has no effect on us. It's kind of like what we do with the "Sell your possessions and give the money to the poor" command we encountered in the last chapter.

Doesn't our constant pursuit of more and costlier things reveal that we really do have a problem with greed? Don't our overflowing closets and garages show that on some level we actually do believe life consists of having abundant possessions? Our large homes and excess accumulation of things are not exactly a subtle tell.

Now, deep down, we probably know it's *not* true that life is about stuff. And it's our disquiet with this common notion that nudges many of us to explore minimalism. But it's not until we start the journey of owning less and begin to experience the freedom of life without too much stuff that we begin to see the full beauty of what Jesus taught about possessions.

Bigger Barns Are Not the Answer

Well, if life doesn't consist in an abundance of possessions, what *does* it consist in? Jesus was getting there.

Immediately after His weighty statement about greed and possessions, He told the crowd a story that started like this:

> The ground of a certain rich man yielded an abundant harvest. He thought to himself, "What shall I do? I have no place to store my crops."
>
> Then he said, "This is what I'll do. I will tear down my barns and build bigger ones, and there I will store my surplus grain. And I'll say to myself, 'You have plenty of grain laid up for many years. Take life easy; eat, drink and be merry.'" (Luke 12:16–19)

If this were all we knew of the story, we might be tempted to think, *Good for him! Isn't that the dream? Make money, get a bigger place, and enjoy life. Besides, what else would this successful farmer do with his extra grain? He needs a bigger barn, a bigger house, a bigger enterprise. His actions are not just expected; they are wise and prudent.*

We might even be conditioned to think this man deserved to enjoy the rewards of his labor. *He built that! His hard work resulted in financial success. He should enjoy it. This story sounds to me like he's living the exact kind of life I might want for myself!*

But look how harshly God speaks to the farmer. "You fool!" He says. "This very night your life will be demanded from you. Then who will get what you have prepared for yourself?" (verse 20).

"Well done, my good and faithful servant" are the words we dream of hearing when we stand face-to-face with the Lord after we die. Not "You fool."

In light of the brevity and uncertainty of life, our plans for selfish comfort provide no guarantee of happiness. Maybe we "get ahead" in the materialistic race for a while, so we start making plans for buying bigger houses, driving nicer cars, or indulging in experiences or substances that give us a good feeling. We may also start thinking about retiring early—about switching from a life of producing value for the world to a life spent mainly just consuming things and enjoying leisure. Yet, sooner or later, our possessions will slip out of our hands, no matter how much we were counting on them, perhaps even as soon as this very night.

I hate to say this, but I hope we're all beginning to realize that the story of the fortunate farmer might resemble our own lives more than we'd like to admit, especially in affluent, developed nations. And once we realize that, Jesus's conclusion to the story should cause us to stop dead in our tracks. He says, "This is how it will be with whoever stores up things for themselves but is not rich toward God" (verse 21).

Whoever. Anyone.

This powerful story is not just for one person or for a group or category of people. It is for everybody—you and me included.

We are not to live life storing up things for ourselves. Instead, we are to be "rich toward God." Now, I'm not sure of everything that being "rich toward God" might entail, but I'm pretty certain it includes at least these two things: desiring God more than we desire money and things, and generously using our earthly wealth in ways that will honor God. And neither of those things can happen if we continue to live as if life consists in the abundance of possessions.

The Cost of the American Dream

For the past few years, Investopedia has tallied how much it costs to live the American dream over the span of an average lifetime. Their most recent estimated figure for a lifetime of living the American dream? A whopping $4.4 million!

In their calculations, they consider eight aspects that are "historically or commonly associated with an ideal yet attainable life in the United States":[2]

1. home ownership
2. new car ownership
3. a wedding
4. raising children
5. providing the children with a college education
6. leisure time, including pets and vacations
7. retirement
8. end-of-life expenses

Again, based on these aspects, Investopedia has determined you would need $4.4 million to live the American dream. And that doesn't even include food, healthcare, insurance, and other "baseline necessities."[3]

You may or may not be surprised by this amount. Yet some of

us might respond by thinking, *If this number is right, then I guess I need to make $4.4 million over the course of my life—because everything on that list is what makes for a good life.*

This is just one example of how society conditions us to focus on ourselves—our own kingdoms, our own pursuits, our own barns. Greed doesn't always look like we picture it; sometimes it just looks like how everyone else is living.

We may have altruistic desires and nonmaterialistic values, but often we think we can combine them with the nice house, the nice car, and all the rest that comes with the American dream. Just like the farmer, we believe we can "have it all," not recognizing that greed is motivating us more than we realize.

Pursuing the American dream has costs—and I'm not talking about the $4.4 million. Greed can play out in our lives far more subtly than we think.

Everyman Greed

After living in Wisconsin for a few years, my family and I moved to Vermont, where I began leading another youth ministry. There I made a friend named Daniel in our new church. A wiry guy with a big smile and short-cropped blond hair, Daniel was fun to hang out with, and we had a lot in common. He and his wife had three boys who were around the same ages as our two kids.

When I first met him, Daniel worked at a construction company, but before long he decided to start his own business as a landscaping general contractor. I admired his initiative and encouraged him in this venture, as did his wife and others.

He was very good at what he did and soon had a lot of people asking for his services. He quickly discovered that as a business owner, the harder he worked, the more money he could make. So, he would work Monday through Friday pretty hard. In a short time, he was bringing in far more money through his business than he had as an employee for someone else. It seemed to verify that he had made the right career move.

An unexpected offer of a big job came up one time, and he reasoned, *I don't really have the time to take this one. But it's just a short-term job and pays well. If I work a few Saturdays, I can get this done. I will make some extra money, and then I will be able to take my family on a wonderful vacation.* So, he took the temporary job and started working on Saturdays.

As it turned out, he kept putting off the family vacation. But with all the extra money he was making, he decided to buy a boat. Finding the time to get away for an extended period was proving too difficult, but with a boat, they could be together all the time. At least that was his rationale.

Now they owned a boat, but as you might guess, they didn't actually use it much. There was always more work to accept—and by now, working on Saturdays had become Daniel's norm. Making the payments on the new truck and trailer he needed to tow the boat required that of him.

One particular Saturday, a few things didn't go his way on the job. He ended up working later than he had planned and returned home exhausted. Daniel told his wife, "I'm so tired. I just need to sleep in tomorrow and skip church so I can refresh for next week. I'm sorry. It's just this one time."

The next day, while his wife took their three boys to church, Daniel got some sleep in their quiet home. He woke up feeling more rested than he had in a while. It was great!

Then he had an idea. *If I start using Sunday mornings to sleep in and get a little paperwork done while the family is at church, I'll free up time during the week and be able to accomplish even more improvement projects.*

Maybe you can picture where this story ends.

Today, Daniel still has his landscaping business, and he's making even more money than when I knew him. But no one has seen him at church in a long time. Even worse, he's now divorced from his wife and sees his boys only every other weekend.

I don't want to single out Daniel for blame. And as a self-employed person myself, I understand the temptations that come with that way of working. But the point of this story is relevant for us regardless of our jobs or wealth: *This* is what greed can look like.

Greed doesn't usually look like a billionaire anchored offshore in their yacht or a hostile takeover specialist dismantling companies to add to their own vast wealth. It's more often regular people—people like Daniel and you and me—making simple choices to put the accumulation of wealth and possessions above more important values. What we think is normal and even admirable might be greed already.

Maybe it's time to do the abnormal.

God's Company

The Barnhart family figured out an abnormal (but very godly) response to increasing income.

"In our society we think of business success as a blessing. I think business success is much more dangerous than failure," says Alan, co-overseer of Barnhart Crane & Rigging, a large Tennessee-based company.[4]

In 1986, when Alan and his brother, Eric, took over the small company their parents had started and began to see that it might grow into a moneymaking powerhouse, they decided to keep clearly in mind that the company and all its proceeds belonged to God. Alan explains, "My job is to be a steward and figure out what God wants me to do with His stuff."

He also decided it was good to have a healthy fear of wealth—that is, a fear that business success could become detrimental to his life and faith. "Dozens of verses . . . brought me to that conclusion," Alan says. "I saw it in other people's lives. . . . Greed is something our enemy uses to twist us around, and that includes believers. And I didn't want it to be my reality."[5]

He and his wife, Katherine, decided early on that they wouldn't ramp up their lifestyle as the business grew. So, they made a radical decision. "We basically broke the connection between our income and our consumption." They originally set their salary at $40,000 per year. It increased to $160,000 during their child-rearing years but is now at $100,000. With boundaries in place, they have never lived extravagantly, but neither have they ever lacked anything necessary. They have modest but adequate retirement savings and feel comfortable with their financial future.

Meanwhile, over the years the company has grown from ten employees to more than a thousand today, with revenues that top $400 million. If the Barnharts aren't taking that money as profit and spending it on themselves, where has it gone?

The first year the Barnhart brothers made money, they gave away around $50,000. It seemed like a huge amount to them at the time. But as the company grew, so would the giving.

Around 2005, they set a goal to give away $1 million per month. That seemed like a stretch, if not an impossibility, given the revenue of their company at the time. But right after they set that goal, the company entered its biggest phase of expansion. They have given away at least a million dollars every month since then, and in one year gave away a total of $21 million.[6] Most of it goes to fund "Christian evangelism, church planting, Christian discipleship, leadership training, and ministering to the poor."[7]

And corporate charitable giving isn't even the end of the story.

Although the Barnharts weren't getting rich off the company, it still didn't feel right for them to own such a large enterprise. The solution they came up with, in 2007, was to give 99 percent of the company to National Christian Foundation, retaining a 1 percent ownership and all the voting rights. Later they would put the 1 percent in a voting trust, meaning they are no longer owners of the company at all, although they still have leadership roles in it. Katherine says this "legally brought us into a position where we already were spiritually."[8]

Barnhart Crane & Rigging continues to thrive, and along with it, numerous ministries around the world are flourishing too.

Now, I'm not sharing this story to say that we should all give away 99 percent of our businesses (although imagine how different the world might look if we did). But to me, the Barnharts exemplify one way of living out the truth Jesus taught us in the parable of the rich fool. A great harvest doesn't have to result in bigger barns.

A Beautiful Future

Pastor Tim Keller said we should all begin with a working hypothesis that greed is an issue for us. "If greed hides itself so deeply, no one should be confident that it is not a problem for them."[9]

This chapter may have helped you identify some greed lurking in your heart. So now picture for just a moment how beautiful your life would become if it were no longer motivated by greed. A life where success isn't measured by your bank account, your home size, or the model of your iPhone. What would that mean for your family, your community, and your church?

I imagine, without the influence of greed on our actions, we would become more available—to our kids, friends, and neighbors. We'd be quicker to listen, help, and give. We would see our financial gain not as an opportunity to accumulate trophies to display but as a tool to bless. Our homes, our time, our money—they would all become available for displaying love. Laying down our lives for others would be easier to achieve.

And all of this, I believe, would look like Jesus to others.

But living this kind of life requires more than overcoming greed. There is another human tendency Jesus mentions in Luke 12. And again, we will find that minimalism helps us overcome it.

7

The End of Anxiety

In Luke 12, where we find the story of the farmer who spent his final night dreaming of building bigger barns, Jesus explains to the people that life is not found in the abundance of possessions. I imagine that the man who initially asked Jesus to settle his inheritance dispute is still standing there. Jesus has refused to settle the dispute, warned against greed, and told the farmer parable. Without stopping, He makes a fascinating transition.

"Therefore I tell you . . ." He says, clearly tying these conversations together. And what does He start talking about? *Worry.*

Isn't that interesting? Because in explaining "this is how it will be with whoever stores up things for themselves but is not rich toward God," Jesus also wants to address fear and anxiety.

Greed rides in tandem with worry.

Here is how this next section of Jesus's teaching begins: "Therefore I tell you, do not worry about your life, what you will eat; or about your body, what you will wear. For life is more than food, and the body more than clothes" (verses 22–23).

Birds and flowers don't worry, points out Jesus, yet God provides for them. So why should we worry? After all, human beings are more valuable to God than the plants and animals. Logically and theologically, that makes a lot of sense. It's even poetic.

Jesus brings His argument to its point like this: "Do not set your heart on what you will eat or drink; do not worry about it. For the pagan world runs after all such things, and your Father knows that you need them. But seek his kingdom, and these things will be given to you as well" (verses 29–31).

To fully understand that life does not consist in the abundance of possessions and to fully participate in a life rich toward God, we must overcome not just greed but also worry. Jesus is talking about an exchange in motivations. Instead of operating out of the usual motivations of greed and worry, we can move to kingdom motivations. We can pursue the things that God cares about, and our needs will be met along the way.

One reason this teaching can be so difficult to comprehend is that we tend to think very differently about worry. While we might know it's not good, surely it's not on a par with something as awful as *greed*, is it?

An Approved Vice

Why would Jesus start a conversation about greed, then immediately talk about worry in the same conversation? Greed and worry fall into completely different categories, don't they?

Indeed, greed and worry *are* different, but they have more in common than we think. Namely, they produce the same negative outcomes in our lives: the *accumulation and possession of more things* for ourselves than we need and, subsequently, the *missed opportunity and joy of giving* to the kingdom of God.

Culturally, worry is more accepted than greed. It is seen as prudent and wise, even thoughtful at times. But don't be fooled; it is likely producing the same result in our lives as greed and selfishness. It keeps our fists tightly clenched on money and possessions.

Social-science researchers are finding that "insecurity—both financial and emotional—lies at the heart of consumeristic cravings." Their research has shown that people who grow up at physical risk, in extreme poverty, or in dysfunctional or divorced families are prone to being more materialistic later in life. One study indicated that "when provoked with thoughts of the most extreme uncertainty of them all—death—people reported more materialistic leanings."[1]

We're concerned about what might happen to us, so one way we try to feel safe is to accumulate things around us—things that seem to hold some value and might help us when circumstances get tough.

Worry also goes along with a scarcity mindset. Many times, I've heard things like "My husband grew up very poor, so it's really hard for him to get rid of things." In the midst of minimizing, we might hesitate, thinking, *What if I need this again sometime? What if I couldn't afford to replace it?*

Greed says, "Eat, drink, and be merry!" Worry says, "Protect, guard, and control." But the result is the same: unnecessary and harmful accumulation of stuff.

Worry may be natural in a world filled with risks when you don't know God who loves you and cares for you. But for people of faith, worry conveys insufficient trust in God—the One who has promised to always look out for us.

Kept in God's Care

When I was in college in Omaha, Nebraska, one of my good friends was a guy named Brian. He had a story I've never forgotten about trusting God enough to put His kingdom first no matter what.

Brian grew up in Illinois in a comfortable home. His dad was an executive at a financial services company, and life was good for the family. But when Brian was a sophomore in high school, everything changed. His dad came home one day and, over dinner, with his supportive wife sitting next to him, informed the three kids he had just lost his job.

Brian's parents were hesitant to share the details, but his mom mentioned how the company had started pushing practices that didn't sit right with his dad—things that he felt were dishonest and unfair. When he'd spoken up repeatedly, he was first passed over for promotions and eventually let go.

"I was nervous about my dad, the sole breadwinner in our family, being out of a job," Brian told me. "Everything changed in a moment. I didn't understand all the details or what it all meant, but I could tell it was a big deal. I only knew he was fired for doing what he believed God would want him to do."

At first, the family cut back on everything—no vacations, no extras, less eating out, even a slimmed-down version of Christmas that year. As a teenager, Brian felt the weight of it. "It was hard," he said. "I never felt like we weren't going to have enough, but our lifestyle definitely changed."

Eventually the firing meant they moved to a new city (Omaha)—right in the middle of Brian's years in high school—so his dad could start over in a different company. As you might imagine, at the time, it felt like just another hard thing to deal with. But looking back, Brian described it as one of the greatest things that ever happened in his life.

At his new high school, Brian met a new group of friends—strong Christians who welcomed him into their group and invited him to church. "Because of their friendship and example, six months after we moved," he said, "I rediscovered Jesus in a new way and committed my life to following Him."

I never knew Brian during that difficult time in his family's life. But his faith inspired me greatly when I got to know him during college, and for that I am thankful.

I share this story with you because, first, it reminds me of Jesus's words in Luke 12:31: "Seek his kingdom, and these things will be given to you as well." When we choose to live with faithful integrity rather than with worry (as Brian's father did), God takes care of us—often providing for us in ways we don't expect.

But even more than that, Brian's story serves as an example that we don't always see the long-term plans God has for our lives. His dad's firing for standing up for what was right, despite the consequences, led to Brian's renewed faith and passion for Christ. That was an outcome unique to their situation, but it illustrates why we don't need to worry when God is taking care of us.

What *do* we do, then? Jesus is going to explain. And if you remember the story of the rich young ruler, it will sound a little familiar.

The Heart Follows

"Sell your possessions and give to the poor," said Jesus. "Provide purses for yourselves that will not wear out, a treasure in heaven that will never fail, where no thief comes near and no moth destroys. For where your treasure is, there your heart will be also" (verses 33–34).

Did you know this is the teaching immediately following Jesus's call to "seek the kingdom?" In Matthew's gospel, it's one of the most well-known verses in all of Scripture: "But seek first his kingdom and his righteousness . . ." In Luke's account, Jesus follows this call with a clear instruction on how to overcome worry: Sell your possessions!

Jesus applies His teaching about not worrying to the areas of our finances and ownership. And that makes sense. Or maybe I should say, once we start actually doing what He said to do, it makes sense.

How do we typically think about being rich toward God? *If I was just in a better place financially, I could give. Right now, I don't know where the money would come from. Or if I did begin giving, I don't know how I'd afford to eat or buy new clothes or pay the rent.* Sometimes it's not even about basic needs. We're worried that if we give too much, we can't eat out as much as we'd like, wear the newest fashions, afford winter ski trips, or buy bigger homes and better cars. All those things are enough to stymie our generosity impulses and keep us from being rich toward God. And we know that to be true because we've all seen it in our own lives, haven't we?

Look at the passage again. It is action that brings the result. It is when we trust God and follow His instruction that we begin to move beyond the fear that makes us hold tightly to our things. A saying widely attributed to Maya Angelou is "We need much less than we think we need." And only when we own less can we learn that we need less.

That's why Jesus said, "Where your treasure is, there your heart will be also." In our minds, we think the opposite is true—that once we care about something, our treasure will follow. In this case, we believe that if we first begin to care supremely about God's kingdom, *then* we'll begin to devote our treasure to His works. But it's actually the other way around: Once we start redirecting our treasure, that will help us get our hearts in the right place.

I have a friend who recently bought Arizona Cardinals season tickets. Can you guess what he begins almost every conversation with now? Yup, the Arizona Cardinals. The moves they made, their new coach, their upcoming schedule, the last game. I know that attending the games regularly is a new thing to him, and it is a natural conversation starter. But I couldn't help but notice that his focus has followed his purchase.

And it made me ask myself what I typically start talking about when someone asks, "What's new with you?"

Believe it or not, my go-to conversation topic is *not* minimalism (that's a close second, though). It's The Hope Effect, the orphan care ministry I started and help fund. I'm often thinking about kids we have placed into loving families, negotiations we are carrying out to help improve orphan care in a new town, or whatever else is currently going on with the organization. That's what's on my heart, so it's what comes out of my mouth first.

In a practical way, our hearts really do end up following our treasure.

How Minimalism Kills Worry

How exactly does minimalism reduce our worry? I can't claim to understand it fully, but I've made a few observations.

Minimalism reveals how little we need.

As we start living with less, we notice that we're doing fine—better, in fact. *I don't need all those clothes to be well dressed and liked by my friends. I don't need all those dishes and that kitchen gear to make joyful meals for my family and our guests. This old car is getting me around just fine, and I don't need to replace it with a newer model anytime soon.*

Soon we find ourselves worrying less and less about having enough stuff. How light it makes us feel!

Minimalism frees us to become more faithful with our resources.

The security we find in hoarding our money and things is fleeting at best. When we look for it there, we always come up short. But a confidence comes from knowing we are living in God's will, being faithful with our resources. It's a confidence that He will care for us because we are right where He wants us to be.

Minimalism provides margin to handle life's uncertainties.

Typically, minimalists have less debt and more savings than they did before owning less. Their schedule is less packed, making it easier to respond to emergencies. They are less distracted, less frazzled, less tired, and more focused, more alert, more at peace. All of this means that minimalists don't have to feel as vulnerable about the trials that will inevitably come along in life.

For people who are overwhelmed by maintaining an overly complicated lifestyle, risks can seem magnified. Minimalists have more confidence that, with God's presence, they can handle whatever they may face.

Minimalism changes our focus.

With minimalism, rather than our hearts being set on all the things we want to get, our minds find rest in the blessings and goodness God has provided for us already. This provision in the present gives us confidence for the future.

The Broken Spatula

An acquaintance of mine, Kathy Perry, told me how she got started on her minimalism journey. It began because she came face-to-face with the problem of worry—and a spatula.

Kathy related this story: "A sweet lady shared at a women's brunch about packing up her home because her pastor husband had been called to missionary work in Africa. She spoke about putting a broken spatula into a box to go to storage while they were gone. And it struck her that here she was trusting God to take her and her two small children to a foreign country but she wasn't trusting that when they came back, He would provide her with a spatula—maybe even one that wasn't broken."

The spatula story got my friend thinking. She realized that she kept or stocked up on things because she didn't quite trust that in the future God would provide what she needed. So, she went home and packed up twenty black sweatshirts that she had randomly bought because "you never know when you might need a black sweatshirt, and what if Walmart runs out?"

That was more than ten years ago, and Kathy has unloaded many, many things since then. But she still asks herself the same question: "If I need this in the future, do I trust that God will provide for my need at that time?"

She's more trusting now, less anxious, and able to live in confidence that God will provide.

Start minimizing and watch how you'll no longer worry so much about needing to hold on to large amounts of money and things.

Motivations Revealed

Do we overcome worry in our hearts and then go on to minimize, or do we start minimizing and then see our worry dissipate? Which comes first?

For Kathy Perry, being confronted with her anxiety problem inspired her to try minimizing. But only over time and with the removal of much of her unnecessary stuff did she really learn trust and make it a habit.

I think that's often how it goes: Minimalism goes first. That was certainly true in the Becker family. As Kim and I began to minimize, it revealed to us the levels of worry in our hearts. The same is true for greed and other unhealthy motivations that self-examination might uncover in our hearts.

We're not alone in these kinds of self-discoveries that come through minimalism.

Zoë Kim, author of *Minimalism for Families,* writes, "As we practice more mindful consumption, we've shared more conversations about the difference between a need and a want. We are more inclined to examine what motivates us, to see where that could lead us, and decide if it's a worthwhile place to go."[2]

The enemy wants to see you worked up and anxious all the time. Jesus invites you to a childlike trust that God is taking care of you, as a loving parent takes care of their young child. Let minimalism move you from worry to uncluttered faith.

I can also testify that as we put our focus on God and trust in Him to provide for us, He proves faithful, and our confidence grows. Made freer by minimalism, we embrace the adventure God is taking us on—life more abundant than excess possessions.

8

Living on Purpose

When I was planning an issue about personal finance for my digital magazine *Simplify*, I reached out to Dr. Kelvin Wong, a professor of economics at Arizona State University, as a potential contributor. As a writing prompt, I asked him, "If you had the entire world in your classroom for eight to ten minutes and you could teach them any lesson you wanted about economics, what is the most important thing you would want everybody in the world to understand?"

Dr. Wong's response might surprise you. He chose to write and teach about the economic principle of opportunity cost. As defined by Investopedia, "Opportunity cost represents the desirable benefits someone foregoes by choosing one alternative instead of another."[1]

In his article Dr. Wong explained the importance this way: "Every choice we make comes with a cost, even those that are monetarily free (ever heard the phrase 'There is no free lunch'?), since even our time or energy can be put to alternative uses."[2]

Whenever you choose to spend your time and money to do

something (such as buy an item or engage in an experience), you're choosing *not* to spend them on everything else they could go toward. That's why economists like Dr. Wong encourage people to stop and think about their consumption choices. Are we choosing what we really want or need the most?

We must confront two realities concerning this concept. First, because we are finite creatures, every decision we make comes with an opportunity cost. And second, we're flawed creatures, so each of us will choose the lesser over the greater sometimes. This is human reality.

Nevertheless, it is sad when we *carelessly* or *repeatedly* make choices to prioritize money and possessions over more important pursuits. This usually happens when we simply go along with cultural assumptions about what's important and never really think through our decisions.

Many times, we don't even realize the full range of the opportunity costs we incur—things like lost significance, lost satisfaction, lost productivity, lost achievement, lost joy, lost independence, and lost relationships. What a tremendous waste!

When our faith is uncluttered through minimalism, we are free to make careful and Christlike decisions about how to use our resources wisely. As I like to say, we are free to be *intentional.* So, we are far more likely to manage our opportunity costs wisely, most often choosing what is better. Doesn't that sound appealing?

It's biblical too. The apostle Paul calls this "making the most of every opportunity."

Make the Most of Every Opportunity

In his letter to the Ephesians, Paul writes, "Be very careful . . . how you live—not as unwise but as wise, *making the most of every opportunity* . . ." (5:15–16). His exhortation is a reminder that we are called to live wisely in a fallen world. The Spirit encourages us to avoid foolishness and instead understand the Lord's will (verse 17), walking in it fully at every opportunity.

To understand the full weight of the instruction, we need to back up to Ephesians 4:20–24, where Paul begins a list of exhortations. In those verses, Paul describes a beautiful reality about those who have chosen to follow Christ. He reminds us that we have put off our old selves (which are being corrupted by deceitful desires); we are made new in the attitude of our minds; and we have put on new selves, "created to be like God in true righteousness and holiness." What a glorious promise—your old self is gone, and a new, better life has come!

Following this beautiful description of our new life in Christ, Paul offers a list of how we should live in light of these amazing truths. He refers to such things as avoiding unwholesome talk, speaking with kindness, and living free from impurity and greed (4:29–5:3). And then, right in the middle of these exhortations about how we should live in our new selves, he tells us to "be very careful . . . making the most of every opportunity." In other words, living an intentional life is as important to God as avoiding sexual immorality, greed, rage, and bitterness. It is given the same weight as husband-wife relationships, parent-child relationships, and our workplace conduct.

"Making the most of every opportunity" isn't just suggested; it is commanded. It is a fundamental call to intentional godliness in our lives. And minimalism helps us live it out.

Now, here's something you may never have known before. In Greek, the term translated "making the most of" (5:16) means "to redeem" or "to buy up."[3] We live in a world where people are eager to take advantage of a great purchase. We celebrate Black Friday or Amazon Prime Day sales. But instead of deals at a department store, Paul encourages us to use our lives to purchase *opportunities.*

But what does it really mean to "buy up" or make the most of every opportunity? It means we take every occasion we're given to intentionally advance God's work in the world wherever and however we can. Each new day is a gift filled with chances to make wise decisions about how to live out God's will. And let me point out something that will help make this goal seem more attainable.

Often we think of opportunities as big, life-changing events: career decisions, major life choices, or grand acts of service. But Paul's instruction in this passage pushes us to look harder. He doesn't say to make the most of just the big decisions in life. He tells us to make the most of *every* opportunity—living wise in the everyday, small moments too.

Every interaction, every conversation, every decision is an opportunity to walk wisely and to do the will of God.

- A conversation with your child at breakfast
- An interaction with the cashier at the supermarket
- A text-message exchange with a friend
- How you choose to spend the first minutes of your morning
- What you watch or listen to as you wind down in the evening
- How you choose to spend the leftover dollars at the end of the month

These might seem insignificant on the surface, but each of these moments is a chance to advance God's kingdom. They are all opportunities to be wise and live out the Lord's will in both our words and our actions.

Minimalism is a powerful tool that can make us more alert to opportunities when they appear and more available to seize them once we recognize them. It's never unwise to start.

A Gift of Perspective

Malia Brown didn't find her way to minimalism through books and blogs. As she puts it, minimalism found her. Sadly, this happened amid one of the worst imaginable circumstances.

"I will never forget the day," Malia wrote me. "My husband and I were sitting in the doctor's office, receiving the news that he had cancer. At that moment, I could not think about anything but nonexistent memories. Not what kind of car we drove, how big our home was, what labels were in the closet, how much was in the checking and savings. All I could think about were the memories we had not shared and might never share."

She and her husband had celebrated special occasions and taken trips together, but she failed to appreciate them and be present in the moment. "Over time, I realized too many memories were about the theme park rides and not the conversations in the line. When it came to dates, I remembered the restaurant, the food, and perhaps how we dressed up, but not the connection and googly eyes shared across the table. The nice vacations, hotels, and excursions were remembered, yet I could not recall a sunrise walk on the beach."

Often, instead of focusing on the moment, she would be thinking about the caption she would use when she posted about the trip, the activity they would do next, the vacation bill they did not save for, or how she needed a promotion to get the upgraded room next time.

Malia reflected, "I thought we had a few decades before we

would be old and gray on the porch, sharing laughs, stories we never shared, or abstract thoughts and dreams. But life can take a different course in an instant. Time is not promised, and we have to live each day making the most of each opportunity provided today."

As her husband began fighting the cancer, Malia started making things easier for the family by minimizing. She couldn't get back the opportunities that had passed by, but by getting rid of their excess stuff, she was able to make the most of the time she had left with her husband before he died. And then, as a single mother, she was able to make the most of her time with her kids.

"I thank God for the gift of perspective in loss and the richest legacy to leave our children, passing down the wealth of minimalism," says Malia today.

Are you ready to build up a lasting wealth of minimalism through being more intentional today?

You Don't Have Time for That

Author Jack Kornfield once wrote, "The trouble is that you think you have time."[4]

This thought routinely spurs me to action and helps me prioritize my life. Because it's true—our priorities often get misplaced specifically because we think we have more time than we actually do.

It's easy to forget the value of every day, especially in a world of constant distraction.

What if we approached life each day fully committed to the reality that time is short? That nothing lasts forever? That tomorrow is promised to no one?

For example, if you knew this was your last year on earth, how would you live differently?

I ask this question not as a downer but as a clarifying lens to focus on what truly matters. Take some time to legitimately answer the question.

In our daily routines, it's easy to get lost in the details and to forget the larger picture. When we do, we spend time on and chase after things that, in the grand scheme of things, hold little significance.

That is why the question above can be so powerfully reframing and why our hearts and minds resonate with it every time we hear it. It reshapes and refines our perspectives almost immediately.

So, I think it would be helpful for each of us to ask ourselves the question again today.

If this were your last year, would you . . .

- redo your countertops?
- buy a new car?
- binge-watch another series on Netflix?
- spend more time at the office?
- acquire more of the latest gadgets?
- obsess over your social media status?
- engage in unnecessary arguments?

Or would it be better to . . .

- prioritize relationships?
- pursue your passions?
- dedicate yourself to activity that brings meaning?
- give generously by sharing your time, resources, and talents with those you desire to bless?

I hope you will intentionally choose more options from the second category. Those are all things we can do daily, regardless of how many days remain in our lives.

Minimalism Can Show You Paths to Intentionality

Scripture presents us with a bold aspiration: "We fix our eyes not on what is seen, but on what is unseen, since what is seen is temporary, but what is unseen is eternal" (2 Corinthians 4:18). For Kim and me, minimalism has been a powerful lens refocusing our attention from the worldly to the heavenly. As we began removing the visible, we could focus better on the invisible.

Based on what we and thousands of others I've met have experienced, I believe minimalism will help *you* find intentionality about things of lasting importance in several areas of life too, including the following:

In your finances

In America, too many people are carrying burdensome debt, living with little cash cushion in case of emergencies, and feeling at a loss when it comes to planning for the future. Minimalism frees up money as well as time and energy you can spend on getting your financial house in order.

Take advantage when minimalism makes it possible for you to become more intentional in this area. Will you pay off student loans? Create a budget? Start paying down your credit cards? Set a savings goal? Increase your giving percentage to 10 percent and hopefully beyond? Make a will?

In your work

The longer you live with fewer possessions, the more your view of money will begin to change. Having a lot of it will become less important to you. Your essential needs will be met, and you will have enough left over to practice generosity—what else is needed?

As your view of money shifts, so will your motivation for work. I believe work will become less about the weekly or biweekly financial deposit and more about the value and contribution you could provide to people's lives. This perspective about money opens the door even wider for honesty, cooperation, people, passion, and joy at work.

Perhaps you will also want to change how you go about working. This might look like going back to school and changing your career focus, starting your own business, negotiating different hours or pay, managing your time differently, working on your leadership or communication skills, or becoming more focused and orderly.

In your health

Six months after discovering minimalism, I faced an upcoming birthday. After spending so many months removing the clutter from our home and life, the last thing I wanted to receive was anything that could become clutter. While brainstorming nonphysical gift ideas, I noticed that a Planet Fitness had just opened down the street from my house. And for the first time, I had the motivation, the finances, and the time to get in better physical shape.

As you minimize, how are you going to make better choices to improve your health? Consider at least the basics: getting an annual physical exam, eating a healthy diet, exercising regularly, keeping your weight in the healthy range, avoiding obviously unhealthy habits (such as smoking), managing your stress, and getting to bed at a reasonable time.

In your relationships

Kim and I discovered that owning less opened the door for new relationships in our lives. We spent less time shopping and cleaning and organizing and started to spend more time with the people who made life enjoyable. We were able to become more involved with our neighbors and our community. We were more willing to have people in our home, as preparing for their arrival became easier. Our capacity for and appreciation of relationships began (and continues) to grow.

Your relationship goals will depend on your starting point. A simpler lifestyle will enable you to think more clearly about your relationships and to work on the areas that are most important to you, such as these:

- If you're married, invest time in this most basic relationship.
- If you're single and want a relationship, put yourself out there to connect with potential dates.
- If you have kids, spend regular time with them to find out what they're thinking and feeling.
- If you're estranged from loved ones, seek reconciliation.
- If you don't know your neighbors, introduce yourself.
- If you're feeling disconnected at church, join a group.
- If you've let friendships languish, initiate get-togethers.

In your values and passions

As I've already defined it, minimalism is the intentional promotion of the things we most value and the removal of everything that distracts us from it. And while this looks different for each person, it always requires its pursuer to further define their passions—and discover intentionality because of it.

You can't decide what to get rid of until you decide what you need to keep. And you can't determine what to keep until you have an idea of what you want to accomplish with your life. Minimalism forces you to answer those questions.

So, for example, a decision as simple as "How many plates are we going to keep?" required my wife and me to restate that hospitality and hosting small groups was important to us.

What about video games? Was that something we were going to keep? Gosh, I do have a bunch of video games—but is that really something I should be spending my time on, anyway?

Be prepared to make specific choices when minimizing raises questions like these for you.

In your spirituality

As I began to realize how much of my thinking had been hijacked by advertisements and a consumer-driven society, I was drawn to the practices of prayer, meditation, and solitude. In the next chapter, we'll be looking at how minimalism can help make your home more of a sanctuary to help you pursue such practices.

But as you get rid of excess, you will find intentionality for a lot of choices around your faith—things like reading and studying the Bible, worshipping, participating in church and ministry, identifying and using your spiritual gifts, becoming a disciple or mentor, and getting counseling or spiritual direction.

If you are in the process of minimizing your home or maintaining minimalism, I hope you will continue with that, because minimalism enables you to take advantage of opportunities. And as you begin practicing greater intentionality, there is one question that I believe can give you clarity in almost every decision.

Is It Beneficial?

"'Everything is permissible'—but not everything is beneficial" (1 Corinthians 10:23).[5] Here, the Holy Spirit points out a truth so significant, there is hardly any area of life it doesn't influence. (To drive home the point, it is raised in the middle of a conversation about food, of all things.)

The truth in 1 Corinthians 10:23 is absolutely profound and life-altering: Because of Christ's sacrifice, I can do anything I want. But some decisions benefit me and the kingdom, and others do not. We are wise, then, to make choices that are worthwhile and constructive as opposed to destructive.

We can spend our money however we want, but some ways to spend it bring greater benefit. Choose those.

We can invest our time however we want, but some ways to invest it bring greater benefit. Choose those.

We can eat or drink anything we want, but some decisions about what we consume bring greater benefit. Choose those.

We can use any words we want with our children or spouses, but some words result in greater benefit. Choose those.

We can pick any entertainment source we want, but some sources have greater benefit. Choose those.

Of course, to help us even more, the Holy Spirit continues, "'Everything is permissible'—but not everything is constructive. Nobody should seek his own good, but the good of others" (verses 23–24).[6]

One question we should continually ask ourselves in making decisions, whether big or small, is this: Does this benefit others?

Because everything may be permissible, but not everything is beneficial.

Choose the Better

When Jesus visited the home of two sisters, one of the young women—Mary—wanted nothing but to sit at Jesus's feet and listen to Him speak. The other sister—Martha—was flustered and preoccupied with the housework. At last Jesus said to this second sister, "Martha, Martha, . . . you are worried and upset about many things, but few things are needed—or indeed only one. Mary has chosen what is better, and it will not be taken away from her" (Luke 10:41–42).

"Mary has chosen what is better."

Some choices in life really are better than others. That's why we need intentionality—the process of discernment for making superior choices and maximizing our impact.

To get a sense of the effort and focus required to live this out, consider that the distracted Martha would almost certainly have agreed that some things in life are worth more of our time than others, yet she still chose incorrectly. And with Jesus in the room!

Intentionality is a skill you can develop over time, and a simplified lifestyle makes it possible. You can learn to choose the *opportunity costs* you would rather bear and position yourself for the *opportunity rewards* you want to reap.

9

Room to Grow

Tania Colley, a teacher who works with Youth for Christ in her native England, was brought up by grandparents who went through World War II. Their example, born out of necessity, taught her to keep everything "just in case."

This approach seemed to make sense to Tania, but by adulthood it had led to her feeling overwhelmed and her husband feeling annoyed because their house was always a mess. A scarcity mindset brought into a world of abundance and affordability often ends with such results.

If people came over to visit, the Colleys would have to move stuff around just to make room for the guests to sit. "It was embarrassing," she told me.

Then COVID-19 hit and the couple began spending even more time at home. Tania decided she could no longer live surrounded by so much stuff. She and her husband began to minimize, using the Becker Method. Each bag that went to charity lifted their spirits and encouraged them to continue.

Yet the consequences of their minimizing went much deeper

than they had anticipated. Tania noted, "Our brains are less frazzled and full, and we have more headspace for God. My bedroom is my place for prayer, and it is now calm, so I feel closer to God."

This benefit provided a new motivation for simple living. She said, "I'm continuing my journey to streamline my connection to God by reducing the interference that clutter brought."

As we saw in chapter 2, Scripture tells us that being too eager for worldly possessions can choke out the Word of God in our hearts and cause us to wander from the faith (Luke 8:7, 14; 1 Timothy 6:10). It stands to reason that the opposite case is true as well: Simplifying our lifestyles can enable us to draw nearer to God, increasing our faith and fruitfulness.

Minimalism frees us to find new opportunities and space in our lives for prioritizing spiritual growth. That is Tania's story—and it can be yours too.

Too Busy for God?

As you look at all you have to do on your calendar, how many times do you catch yourself groaning or complaining out loud, "I'm so busy"? You're far from alone in this feeling of being overscheduled. According to one survey, 60 percent of U.S. adults say they at least sometimes feel too busy to enjoy life, and 12 percent say they feel this way all or most of the time.[1]

What, specifically, is taking up so much of our time? Aside from sleep and paid work, one of the biggest categories is shopping and housework. Want to have your mind blown? According to studies, on average we spend *two hours per day* buying things and taking care of the things we already own.[2]

Have you ever been in a group setting and been asked the

discussion question "If you had one extra hour in your day, how would you spend it?" Well, according to the research results I just mentioned, that doesn't have to be a hypothetical question. You literally can have an extra hour or two in your day if you minimize!

But when we're overbusy making and spending money and managing our possessions, something has to give. For believers, sadly, our pursuit of quality time with God often gets squeezed out first.

Today, less than half of Christians read the Bible as much as once a week.[3] In fact, by the year 2022, America had reached an all-time low for Bible reading.[4] There seems to be an inverse ratio between the time we spend tending to our possessions and the time we spend reading God's Word.

Meanwhile, around 60 percent of Christians pray daily,[5] although most prayers last less than a minute. Busyness is the reason Christians most often cite for not praying more.[6]

One psalm compares the desire to be in the presence of God to extreme thirst.

> As the deer pants for streams of water,
> so my soul pants for you, my God.
> My soul thirsts for God, for the living God.
> When can I go and meet with God? (Psalm 42:1–2)

A lot of us are thirsting for God yet not taking the time to drink more than a few drops at a time.

We ask ourselves, *When can I go and meet with God?* and then answer, *Maybe after I get back from Costco.* Or, *When I'm done with this part-time job I took to pay off the credit cards.* Or, *If I have time after I straighten up the mess in the living room before my mother-in-law comes over.*

Let me point out that none of us is as pressed by responsibilities as Jesus was when crowds swarmed to Him for healing and for the words of life. Yet Jesus knew His soul's need and repeatedly got away to be with His Father in prayer (Mark 1:35; Luke 5:16).

There may be many strategies for reducing busyness, such as cutting back on commitments and setting more boundaries. But for most of us, the *single most attainable way* to decrease busyness and then to secure our time gains *permanently* is to minimize our possessions.

Of course, becoming less busy won't in itself guarantee that we will spend more time in God's presence. (What a waste if we employ our new freedom for something like endless phone swiping!) But it will at least eliminate an obstacle to a life of devotion. If our souls are really panting for God, we must go to Him for the living water that will satisfy our thirst.

Never settle for excessive busyness as "normal" if it's keeping you from what's most important—knowing, loving, and becoming more like Jesus. Imagine turning your home into a sanctuary of calm, where your thoughts can naturally turn toward your Savior.

Turning Down the Volume on Visual Noise

If you've ever gone on a spiritual retreat to a monastery or convent, you know how these spaces tend to be peaceful, clean, and uncrowded as the members of the religious orders go about their daily routines. This is uncluttered faith in an uncluttered space. The monks and nuns purposefully own less so they can focus more of themselves on God.[7]

I am not saying you should become a monk or nun. But we can sure stand to learn a lesson or two from their example, don't you think? They've acquired wisdom in simplicity over the centuries that their orders have existed. And anyway, doesn't a possible connection between a sparsely furnished, minimally decorated space and a mind set "on things above, not on earthly things" (Colossians 3:2) simply make sense?

Too often, though, our clutter creates "visual noise." We look around our homes and see books and knickknacks crowding our shelves, unwashed dishes on our countertops, or baskets of unfolded laundry on our floors, and our brains receive stimuli, just as if we were listening to street noise at a busy corner or the noises of a crowd at a ballpark.

The negative effects of visual noise are well known. It hinders our ability to concentrate, slows our learning, and contributes to fatigue.[8]

And what about its impact on our spiritual lives?

Imagine you are having your daily Bible reading and prayer time and are trying to settle your spirit and focus your mind on God, all while the contents of your room are screaming at you for attention. In a direct way, your possessions could be drawing you away from the spiritual life.

How sad that trinkets manufactured in the world around us would pull us from the Spirit's voice in our lives.

Reducing visual noise in your home can help you and your family members throughout the day. I especially encourage it for people who work at home. And for people who want to have homes that are conducive to worship and prayerfulness, it is essential.

The only way to reduce visual noise is to keep fewer things around. Remove possessions, and turn your attention to the things of God. That's what Judy Hindes did.

Hearing God More Easily

Judy discovered the freedom of minimalism unexpectedly while on vacation in Portugal. She rented a vacation home and couldn't get over the calm feeling she got from the minimalist style. It seemed to her that she could think so much more clearly and with less effort.

"It occurred to me that my brain was unencumbered, and I was more creative," she says. "My brain had a place to think."

Judy pondered how she could re-create this experience at her home in Fresno, because she didn't want the feeling to end.

After returning from her trip, she began the journey to transform her house into a place of calm where she could hear herself think. She started in her bedroom and eventually made her entire home free of clutter and unnecessary stuff.

"I can see the benefits in my spiritual life," she told me with excitement. "I've learned that I can hear God much easier when my surroundings are not full of clutter, distractions, and projects needing to be completed. My surroundings are not competing with my time with God."

But that's not all. She continued, "I feel that my simplified lifestyle provides not only more time available to clearly hear God, but I'm also better equipped to take action and complete whatever He wants me to do. I'm not weighed down and can respond properly, as I was created to be. When I'm not encumbered with senseless stuff, I find the time and energy to respond to what God wants me to do."

That trip to Portugal turned out to be life-changing for Judy in ways she had never anticipated. Her spirituality will never be the same.

"I don't ever want to live in a situation when the stuff around me keeps me from a nearness with God."

Let all the brothers and sisters say, "Amen."

Detaching from the World

Minimalism does more than clear physical space in our homes and remove distractions to our devotional efforts—it also clears space within our hearts for God to speak to us. As we intentionally own less, we begin to detach from the world and its empty promises. And this has a profound impact on preparing our hearts and minds to hear from God.

The physical act of removing the world's influences brings about emotional and mental change. It helps us see, with fresh eyes, how much of our time and energy have been consumed by things that do not fulfill or last very long. It helps us better recognize the empty promises of the world by forcing us to stand face-to-face with wasted time and money. And it opens us up to remember that our lives and days are created for better things than this world can offer.

In that shift, our hearts become better prepared and more desirous of pursuits that actually can fulfill. When we loosen our grips on material things, the world loosens its grip on us. The less we chase after physical possessions, the more we naturally turn our attention to what will last.

Writing to me one day, minimalist Ann O'Neill said, "As I have embraced minimalism, I have become less earthly minded and more spiritually focused. I carefully manage both my time and my money, putting them both to the best use. Worship and service to the Lord are far more valuable and rewarding than any earthly treasures I once sought.

"Earthly goods can weigh heavy as they consume time, energy, and resources that could be invested elsewhere. It has been completely freeing to change my mindset, declutter my home and my lifestyle, and free myself to pursue what is most pleasing to my Lord."

From Conforming to Transforming

But how do we live like this? Paul provides an answer: "Do not conform to the pattern of this world, but be transformed by the renewing of your mind" (Romans 12:2).

Avoiding conformity to the world means resisting the pressures and patterns around us that lead us away from God. It's choosing not to adopt the values, behaviors, and priorities of a fallen culture, whether that be in where we search for wisdom, how we spend our free time, or what we choose to accumulate.

Transformation, on the other hand, is a work of renewal—a complete reorientation of our minds and hearts through the power of the Holy Spirit.

As you know, this process isn't instant. It requires time, effort, focus, and discipline. It is found through the practices of daily engaging with God through Scripture, prayer, and solitude and of regular fellowship with other believers. This is what renews our minds. It's making intentional choices to prioritize God's truth over the world's lies and aligning our thoughts and actions with His will.

And the promise of this verse? It's incredible: "Then you will be able to test and approve what God's will is—his good, pleasing and perfect will."

Have you ever asked, "What is God's will for my life?" This verse holds the answer! When we refuse to conform and we intentionally pursue transformation, God's will becomes clear. He reveals His perfect plans for us—plans that are good, pleasing, and ultimately for our best.

And this transformation becomes much easier when we intentionally remove the patterns (and possessions) of this world from our lives.

Redemption of the Evening

Scripture has been a part of my life since childhood. But my daily discipline of spending time alone in the Word really began in high school when I began taking Christ's call to follow Him more seriously. After school, I would go up to my room and spend time reading and writing in my Bible.

During college, I continued to regularly spend time in the Word—although not as consistently and passionately as those days in high school, I must admit.

When I got into pastoral work, Bible study again became a big part of my life. Partly this was because of my desire for personal devotion, but other times I spent studying the Word simply because I was scheduled to preach that weekend and had a sermon to write!

I wish I could say that my personal discipline of being in the Word steadily strengthened throughout my life. But unfortunately, that was not the case.

I don't want to overstate the direct connection in this next sentence, because I know there were other factors in play. But looking back now, I can see that the more complicated life got with kids, houses, cars, technology, and worldly distractions, the less frequent my daily devotions became.

I would still squeeze in time for personal devotions, but it wasn't as regular or as long as it once had been. When I prayed, I would often be distracted by thoughts of things I needed to do around the house or in my work. I would think about something that I needed to pick up for the kids or Kim. It made me antsy and kept me from concentrating on what was important in the moment. In retrospect, it's not surprising that my relationship with Jesus was feeling stale.

This was a frustration in my life, but it was *not* one of the frustrations that helped push me into minimalism. That's because I didn't at first see a connection between my problem with owning too much stuff and my faltering devotional life. Most of us don't. But I can see it now. Truly, though, it came as a surprise to me when my spirituality got a rebirth after my wife and I began minimizing.

As you've seen in this book, there are countless overlaps between our physical possessions and spiritual journeys. But one specific change because of minimalism sparked a renewal in my personal devotional life.

We got rid of our televisions.

When we discovered minimalism, our kids were six and three. We owned four televisions, one each in our living room, kitchen, bedroom, and basement. The average American home contains more television sets than people, so we were not alone in having more TVs than we really needed.[9]

Before minimizing, Kim and I would typically sit down to watch TV after putting the kids to bed early in the evening. We would be exhausted but not yet ready for sleep. After minimizing, though, I started using my evenings differently.

Eight months into our minimalist journey, we got rid of all our TVs except one. We also got rid of our cable service. And those decisions inspired a change in me that I never would have predicted. I now had space and passion to again spend consistent time in the Word. It also prompted me to not just read the words but also journal the lessons I was learning.

Regularly, each week, I would intentionally spend time in the evenings revisiting and meditating on some of the lessons and spiritual changes that were taking place in my life.

Who knew that getting rid of extra TVs would lead to me being transformed by the renewing of my mind, conforming less to the pattern of this world and more to the image of Christ?

Maybe that is why Tania's and Judy's stories resonate so much with me—my story is the same.

Seek and Find

In a *Relevant* article, Annie Eisner said, "Decluttering is about letting go of the things that pull you away from the life God has for you. It's a small, physical act with big, spiritual implications. By clearing out our homes, we create room for peace and clarity—and that reflects in our souls. When we let go of what's unnecessary, we can focus on what truly matters: our faith, our relationships, and our purpose."[10]

Samantha Medina (whom we'll meet again in a future chapter) is a minimalist whose experience of the spiritual benefits of owning less has been like so many others. "This is not something I'm sure anyone wants to admit," she said, "but I fell into that trap of allowing items and possessions to consume my time and energy, leaving nothing for Christ. Being around too much stuff, I felt like I had to push down my relationship with Christ while I took care of everything externally. Since living in a minimalist home, I have been able to read my Bible since there are no chores to do and no stuff piled up. I am still recovering from all the time spent on dealing with stuff and not on Christ, but each day it gets better and the contentment with Christ grows."

Are you reading this chapter at home? If so, look at your surroundings and ask yourself whether they are as conducive to keeping your mental focus on God as they could be. What would a more devotion-inspiring interior look like? Consecrate your home to the service of God, because the benefit could hardly be higher.

You see, obeying Jesus's call to get rid of our unnecessary possessions has many rewards, and the greatest of these is God Himself.

These loving words of the Lord—first delivered to the Jews in Jeremiah's day—are for you too: " 'I know the plans I have for you,' declares the LORD, 'plans to prosper you and not to harm you, plans to give you hope and a future. Then you will call on me and come and pray to me, and I will listen to you. You will seek me and find me when you seek me with all your heart' " (Jeremiah 29:11–13).

If we seek God, we will find Him—and along with Him, all the blessings He so longs to give us. Reducing the interference caused by our clutter and streamlining our connection to God through minimizing our possessions are proven ways to start enjoying a new level of communion with God.

10

People over Possessions

"Twins? Are you kidding me?"

That was the understandable reaction of Julie Sieben of Hastings, Minnesota, and her husband, Todd, when their ob-gyn informed them that Julie was carrying twin girls. They already had one toddler at home.

"Floods of emotions filled my mind," recalls Julie. "Fear. Worry about financial strain. Excitement. Shock. And of course, pure joy."

Thirty-four weeks into her pregnancy, Julie was put on bed rest and had to take leave from her job as a kindergarten teacher. Two weeks later, the babies were born. After a few days under observation at the hospital, the little girls—Greta and Violet—came home.

"That's when the reality of having twin newborns set in," says Julie. "It didn't take long for this tired mama to become overwhelmed. I have always been organized, but adding two babies to our family brought so much stuff into our home, and I couldn't keep up."

Julie turned to minimalism to improve the situation. She cleaned out a drawer, then a closet, then a dresser, and slowly worked her way through their home.

Being the mom of three little ones would inevitably be challenging. The feeling of overwhelm came back from time to time, as to be expected. But having a simplified, uncluttered house got the Siebens through, enabling them to take care of and enjoy their three young blessings.

When I asked her to tell me about the connection between minimalism and raising her children, she said, "I was surprised at how owning less stuff allowed me to be a more present mother and wife. Owning less was the only significant change we made—but it made a world of difference in our relationships as a family."

Only about 3 percent of us will ever be like the Siebens (and my own parents) and know what having twin babies is like. But whether each of us is raising young children, joining a small group, getting to know the parents of our teenager's new best friend, spending time with our softball team, or just making time to meet the neighbors or a co-worker, we have to make choices about prioritizing people over stuff.

If we're in what we might call a *high possessions, high people* state (that is, we have lots of things *and* lots of relationships), we can be run ragged trying to give adequate attention to both kinds of responsibilities. The consequences (as with Julie Sieben) almost inevitably are exhaustion, stress, and feelings of inadequacy.

Some people opt to go *high possessions, low people.* They refuse to give up their stuff (or their desire for it), even when it means having less room in their lives for relationships. I find this sad.

Going *low possessions, low people*—and I encounter more misanthropic minimalists than you might think—isn't much better.

Yet there is another option: *low possessions, high people.*

More stuff could never bring us as much happiness as more closeness with other people. Let's do what Julie did and live with fewer material goods so we can prioritize our family, neighbors, co-workers, bosses, teachers, mentors, customers, teammates, fellow church members, old friends, and new friends, as well as the people we minister to and even strangers whom God has yet to bring into our lives.

As Jesus taught us, love of neighbor is second only to love of God in importance (Matthew 22:34–40). I have written quite a bit in other chapters about how minimalism can spark our relationship with Christ; here I am going to focus more on the profound and positive effects of minimalism on our relationships with other people.

More people to love and more people to love you—who doesn't want that? Again, we find this is part of the abundant life that comes through embracing and living out Jesus's teachings on money and possessions.

A Religion of Relationship

I'm an introvert by nature. Don't get me wrong—I love attention (maybe more than is healthy), and I love being on stage and talking to people. But at the end of the day, I need to get away by myself for inner restoration.

So, I can personally attest that different people have different capacities for relationship. Also, different circumstances and seasons of life bring different degrees of relational intensity and opportunity. But for anyone who follows Christ, people will always in some way be a priority. After all, relationship is at the heart of the Christian faith.

Before creation, the Father, Son, and Holy Spirit dwelt together in the Trinity from eternity past. Relationship has forever been a part of the truest reality there is.

Then God shared the gift of relationship when He created Adam and walked in the Garden of Eden with him. God also knew Adam needed human companionship, saying it was "not good for the man to be alone" (Genesis 2:18), so He made Eve. The first couple set a pattern, such that ever afterward, "a man leaves his father and mother and is united to his wife, and they become one flesh" (verse 24).

The story of the sin in the garden is one of Adam and Eve breaking their relationship with God. And the consequences were passed down to all succeeding generations. To resolve our sin problem, God sent His Son, Jesus, to offer His life to restore that relationship for any who would accept the gift by faith.

When Christ left the earth, He sent His Spirit to dwell among us and established His church so that believers, again in relationship with one another, could serve as Christ's ambassadors to bring even more people to Him. The importance of relationship in God's design can also be seen throughout the rest of the New Testament—just look at how many verses teach us how to interact with others and do relationship better.[1]

The grand narrative of the Bible begins in a garden but ends in a city, the New Jerusalem. And the greatest difference between a garden and a city is the people, in relationship with one another, who inhabit it.

These are amazing and fundamental truths, and it's good to be reminded of them—but am I saying much to you that you've never heard before? I doubt it. We already know that Christianity is a religion of relationship, don't we?

So, why do we often live our lives more focused on acquisition and possession of material things than on relationship?

I think consumerism is one of the ways Satan distracts us from our purpose and our joy. He uses a materialistic culture to keep us from the very reason we were created. He convinces us that our lives will be happier, people will like us better, we'll fit in the right crowd, and our influence will expand if we have more and own the right things. He deceives us into thinking that the best way to live an abundant life is to accumulate more and that it is okay if our ever-increasing piles of possessions demand more and more of our time. And we fail to realize how all our possessions (and the pursuit of even more) are keeping us from relationship.

The world's clamor of consumerism is loud. Meanwhile, Jesus is quietly calling us out of all that.

Leave Your Nets

Jesus's way of doing ministry was in a group. He gathered a group of disciples—a circle of relationships—around Him. And He chose each of the Twelve prayerfully and intentionally.

Two young fishermen, brothers named Andrew and Simon Peter, had already met Jesus through the great minimalist John the Baptist. So when Jesus showed up on the shore one day while Andrew and Peter were fishing with a net, they must have been excited to see Him again.

"Come, follow me," Jesus called out to them (Matthew 4:19).

And they did. Immediately. The story says they "left their nets and followed him" (verse 20).

Actually, if you think about it, they must have left not only their nets but also nearly all their possessions.

They left the security and predictability of having jobs in the family fishing business.

They left a steady income and what it could buy them.

They left their homes and all their contents, comforts, and familiarity.

Probably they took with them no more than they could wear on their backs or carry in their hands.

We could say they underwent a sudden, radical minimalism when they left it all behind to follow Jesus. And why? Jesus had invited them to something better: "I will make you fishers of men" (verse 19, NKJV).

They would be living with Jesus and the other disciples and mixing with crowds as they helped Jesus in the supreme cause of netting souls. They left their possessions to pursue a ministry of relationships.

What a powerful example of prioritizing people over things that we should all seek to emulate in our lives! I almost feel like I could end the chapter right here. But I won't; I have more to say about this.

For instance, I wonder what Peter might have been thinking later in Jesus's ministry when Jesus issued the command "Come, follow me" to another young man. We looked at this incident (Luke 18:18–25) already in chapter 5.

Jesus made it a condition that the rich young ruler sell all he possessed and give the money to the poor before following Jesus. Because of this, the young man made a different decision than the one Peter and Andrew had made. He decided against giving up what he had and following Jesus.

When the young man walked away sad, Peter exclaimed to Jesus, "We have left all we had to follow you!" (verse 28).

As we've seen, there's always a promise attached to God's commands. Jesus detailed the promise attached to His "follow me" command—and it was huge!

"'Truly I tell you,' Jesus said to them, 'no one who has left home or wife or brothers or sisters or parents or children for the sake of the kingdom of God will fail to receive many times as much in this age, and in the age to come eternal life'" (verses 29–30).

The rich young man chose to keep his stuff. Peter and the disciples had given up theirs to invest in people and souls, and their decision would result in receiving "many times as much in this age" and an inheritance of "eternal life" in the age to come. Not a bad trade, if you ask me!

For us, "leaving our nets," as the fishermen disciples did, can stand for all we give up to follow Jesus and put relationships before things. Those relationships won't always be easy. But the reward Jesus promised is for us too. Imagine an exponential return for all we discard—and eternal life to boot!

How Minimalism Helps Our Relationships

Did you know it's been proven that loneliness leads to materialism *and* that materialism reinforces loneliness?[2] Get yourself out of that trap.

To help, let's consider the ways minimalism can improve our relationships.

Frees up time and money

As you already know by now, being minimalist means we spend less time cleaning and organizing and managing and shopping and returning purchases. That freed-up time is a valuable resource we can spend on more important and rewarding purposes, including hanging out with new acquaintances or closer friends or family.

A leisurely hike with a friend is so much more valuable than a trip to the dollar store.

Playing a game with your grandson is better than dusting roomfuls of furniture and decorative items.

Getting to know the new neighbors is more rewarding than repairing the boat you rarely use.

Playing catch with your boy in the backyard is better than cleaning out the garage on a Saturday morning.

Along with available time, you should also have more disposable income after minimizing. Invest your financial savings into relationships with people. In other words, because you've got the money, buy a coffee for a friend. Or go out for dinner or a show or a date.

Redirect your money as well as your time away from physical possessions and toward meaningful experiences with other people.

Reduces stress

Living with clutter is stressful.[3] It's been shown that even *thinking* about a cluttered home raises stress levels.[4]

And we know that being stressed has serious side effects that can impact our relationships, including increased irritability, emotional withdrawal, and argumentativeness.[5] Research has even shown that stress can be passed from one person to another like a contagious disease.[6] Stress is terrible for relationships! It impacts both parties.

Stress can even bring about premature death by contributing to heart disease, elevated blood pressure, obesity, and other conditions that are linked to mortality.[7] If you care about being there for your loved ones, why wouldn't you be interested in reducing stress?

Minimizing may be one of the easiest ways to lower your stress. Without clutter in your life, you will be more available, in both quality and quantity of time, to friends and family and more open and free and appealing in your interactions with others.

Boosts confidence

I can't tell you how many times I've heard people say that they are embarrassed by their clutter. They aren't comfortable when friends come over, because there's so much stuff around the house. Maybe they stop inviting others to their homes entirely.

This loss of hospitality is heartbreaking to me. And it's so unnecessary, if we will just declutter and decide to own only what we need.

I've also observed that when people align their lifestyles with their values through minimizing, they tend to be less secretive. That is, they aren't tempted to mask out-of-control consumer debt or hide problems with overaccumulation. So, they are more open and authentic with others. This, too, is a form of confidence that improves relationships.

Helps us be emotionally present

If we minimize, we have less to distract us from others. We aren't focusing on buying or maintaining stuff, so we can focus on the people in front of us. We can put our attention on more important things.

According to research, minimalists report an increase in meaningful exchanges with family and friends. One parent interviewed for a study said of her relationship with her young son, "I just notice more. . . . Because I'm so part of his play now . . . he'll ask for stories about what we've done that day and I can tell them because I was present."[8]

All of us, regardless of age, love to have calm, attentive friends or loved ones be present with us.

Inspires us to give experiential gifts

Once people declutter, they almost always look at gift giving differently. Instead of giving or asking for *things*, they prefer *experi-*

ences. Escape rooms, hot-air balloon rides, dinners, spa visits, baseball games, green fees, movie passes, museum memberships, art classes—these kinds of things can become more welcome gifts than material goods because they don't add to clutter.

Wouldn't you know it, according to data published in a consumer research journal, experiential gifts are more effective than material gifts at strengthening relationships.[9] Even if you as the giver do not share in the experience, the recipient will think of you before, during, and after the event, promoting a potentially stronger connection than a physical item would.

Spontaneous Hospitality

We all discover different points of view with our spouses when we get married. One surprise Emily Penner of Alberta, Canada, got after her wedding to Errol was to learn he expected they would open their home to guests once a week, if not more frequently.

Emily had been raised in a home where hosting visitors was rare and seen as burdensome. Her family would spend days cleaning the house before guests came over. So, her husband's expectation of regular hospitality came as a shock to her. It seemed completely unrealistic.

Then the couple undertook decluttering.

"I was always labeled by family, teachers, and others as 'messy,'" says Emily. "But after getting rid of more than 60 percent of our household, I found out that the problem was I just held on to too much!" (I hear reports like that all the time.)

Emily and Errol now need only thirty minutes, and often less, to have their home ready for guests. It is not uncommon for the

Penners, as they are leaving church, to invite someone to join them at their home for lunch. Emily is also comfortable with friends dropping in unannounced. Just as her husband had desired, they have guests over practically every week. Before minimizing, she never thought this would be possible—but it is.

Emily says, "I'm really learning to be hospitable spontaneously, and I love it!"

Despite the introversion I have already confessed to, I can easily relate to Emily's excitement over how minimalism opens up a more relational lifestyle.

Bros on Snow

On a November evening in 2013, I was sitting in my living room when I received a text from a new acquaintance, Brian Gardner.

By this time, I had been running Becoming Minimalist for five years and had met many other minimalists online through our shared interests. Brian was launching a new website called No Sidebar that intersects with many of the same themes as Becoming Minimalist. We began emailing back and forth, usually with opportunities and ideas to grow our websites. In fact, I eventually worked on three side projects with Brian: *Simplify Magazine*, *Simple Money Magazine*, and the Clutterfree app.

At this point, though, Brian and I were just starting to become good friends. His text—sent both to me and to a mutual friend—read:

> Hey guys, random idea. I'm going to be in Denver for a week in December. Do you want to meet me there and do some skiing? My Airbnb has plenty of space.

It was a perfect moment of minimalism's benefits bubbling up in my life. I was home on a weekday evening, with no housework or errands on my list. We didn't have much excess money in our bank accounts, but we had some because we had cut our expenses to such a degree. So while in the past this kind of last-minute adventure probably wouldn't have been possible, now it was.

Within ten minutes of receiving the text, after discussing it with Kim, I replied to Brian:

I'm in.

Soon afterward, our other friend texted his agreement as well. We then added a fourth who merely saw our ensuing conversations on social media.

And our first "brocation" was born.

By the second year, eight guys met in Breckenridge, Colorado, for this now-annual skiing trip.

Over the years since, as life has continued to change for all of us, these bros have become some of my closest friends. Through my times with them, I have learned lessons about business, marriage, and life. Many of my most effective business strategies for Becoming Minimalist have come from these trips and the men on them. The relationships have helped me grow in how I approach my health and time management and even how I vacation with my family.

All that to say, I needed relationships like this more than I thought. Most of us do.

Minimalism made them possible.

Yes, I know that lots of people go on annual trips with "the guys" or "the girls" and don't practice minimalism. Many people living materialistic lives have good friends and relationships too. But in my life, some of my closest relationships and most cherished memories are a direct result of minimalism's impact and opportunity.

Minimalism's Advantages for Families

If you have a spouse and/or kids at home, the most important relationships of all are under your own roof. And no doubt, you sense the urgency and responsibility to be a loving spouse and an intentional parent. But in a world filled with distractions, it's easy to let the demands of stuff pull us away even from the people who matter most. There are, of course, other distractions and temptations that can keep us from best loving the families under our roofs, but physical possessions are an often overlooked but controllable one.

Here are some practical ways minimalism benefits a family:

Less stress and distraction

Ellen Galinsky, author of *Mind in the Making* and co-founder of the Families and Work Institute, asked the children of a thousand families, "If you were granted one wish about your parents, what would it be?"

You might guess they would answer, "Spending more time with them." That is what a majority of parents predicted the response would be. But they were wrong.

"The kids' number one wish was that their parents were less tired and less stressed."[10]

Children might be more connected to their parents' emotional state than you'd think. "Studies have shown that parental stress weakens children's brains, depletes their immune systems, and increases their risk of obesity, mental illness, diabetes, allergies, even tooth decay."[11]

Clutter and excess are significant sources of stress within families. Through minimalism, with fewer possessions to manage, there's less to clean, organize, maintain, and buy. And when we're less stressed, we're more patient, more attentive, and more emotionally available for our spouses and children.

More time

Time is the most precious resource we have, and minimalism gives us more of it. This can be seen in no more important place than our families.

Ask any parent of an older child and they will tell you the same thing—time flies. As the saying goes, "The days feel long, but the years are short." We get eighteen summers, twelve times to play Santa, twenty loose teeth, one first day of kindergarten, twelve spring breaks, six months of a driver's permit, one first date, two proms, one graduation . . . and only one childhood in which to communicate our values before they choose their own life.

It's simple: The more time parents spend with their kids, the better off the kids are.[12] And couples who spend more time talking with one another have happier marriages and more intimacy too.[13] So don't overlook the fact that owning less allows you to be more available and more present for your family.

A better example for our kids

James Baldwin once wrote, "Children have never been very good at listening to their elders, but they have never failed to imitate them."[14] Our actions speak louder than our words, and minimalism sets a powerful example for our children.

Recently I spoke at a local university. During the Q&A portion, a professor in the back raised her hand and asked this question: "How do we keep our kids from always wanting more and more stuff?"

I answered, "We model that for them. If our kids are raised in a home where Amazon is delivering a package every couple days or we have so much stuff in our garage that we can't park in it, the message will be received loud and clear: Keep on buying!"

On the other hand, by embracing a life content with fewer possessions, we model important truths: Worldly possessions are not the key to happiness; security is found in Christ and our character; and the pursuit of happiness runs on a different road than where the world is chasing it.

Better use of our money

No one will know how you use your money better than your family. If it is being wasted or treated irresponsibly, it is your family who will notice first *and* suffer the most.

Minimalism provides a better path. It allows us to practice generosity, supporting organizations and people. And the greatest joy in being generous with our money is getting to share with our kids where our dollars go and what they are used for.

Minimalism also teaches financial responsibility. By carefully considering our purchases, we show our kids how to live within their means, avoid debt, and prioritize needs over wants. These small lessons will serve them well as they grow into adulthood.

Greater intentionality

Our homes serve a purpose in our lives—they act as places of rest and as launching pads to make a difference in the world. Minimalism helps us be intentional with the items we bring into our homes, which models intentionality in our spaces, our habits, and our lifestyles.

This mindset quickly extends beyond possessions. Intentionality in our possessions leads to us asking questions of intentionality about the time we spend in other activities and the influences we allow into our lives.

Deep-Spirited Friends

The Message paraphrase of the opening verses of Philippians 2 goes like this: "If you've gotten anything at all out of following Christ, if his love has made any difference in your life, if being in a community of the Spirit means anything to you, if you have a heart, if you *care*—then do me a favor: Agree with each other, love each other, be deep-spirited friends" (verses 1–2).

If we've received any good thing from Jesus (and of course we have, in bucketfuls), the least each of us can do is be a good friend.

God has lavished His love on us because He wants relationship with us. He has placed us in the family of faith. He has sent us into the world to seek out the lonely and the lost on His behalf. We should welcome any means to upgrade our capacities for relationships, and minimalism is one of the most powerful available.

Choose to prioritize relationships.

Remember, the joy equation is *low possessions, high people.*

11

Success Redefined

Demelza Soumagnas, a British missionary, and her French husband, Maxime, first became interested in minimalism in 2016 when they moved into a small flat outside Paris. They were preparing to plant a church, and with this new work plus the demands of parenting their two small boys, they were feeling overwhelmed.

Demelza wrote to me, "I started reducing, sorting, donating, selling, getting rid of stuff to make space for what was important: relationships and time with family, neighbors, and church family."

Six years later, they were living in Bordeaux, in another small apartment, now with three children. This was when world events intervened to show the Soumagnases the value of minimalism on another level. War broke out in Ukraine, and soon Ukrainian women and children were arriving at the Bordeaux train station with nothing and nowhere to go.

"Within days, the first families started arriving. They had small children and they had lost everything. One lady arrived without her glasses. They were shell-shocked. They had no bed, no clothes, no French."

Demelza began bringing refugees to her home. They would enjoy a hot meal; the children would play together; and Demelza would listen to their stories and grieve with them. She and the members of a group she helped form would offer beds, clothes, birthday parties for children—whatever was needed.

"Over those first few months of the war," said Demelza, "I was so grateful that we had space in our home, our energy reserves, our hearts free to do what needed to be done. That space was filled with deep and meaningful conversations, with new friends, with increased humility about what we have.

"It all started with the Lord setting me on the path of minimalism six years ago. At first I thought the decision was just about making my home easier to manage. But now I can see that God was preparing us to look at the purpose of our home and the opportunity of my life in a whole new way."

She ended with this: "To the world we may look poor, but we are some of the richest people in Bordeaux because we know the God who made us and His Son who died for us."

Minimalism helps us achieve success. But before it does that, it teaches us to redefine our concepts of success. Minimalism, coupled with faith in Christ, helps us see that the world's usual measure of doing well—the accumulation of more and more wealth and possessions—is even more inadequate than we suspected. Best of all, we begin to learn that the greatest fulfillment and joy can be found in embracing God's definition of our success: a life spent looking more and more like His Son and contributing to His eternal kingdom.

The Greatest Fear

Early in my own journey toward minimalism, I stumbled on a quote in Francis Chan's book *Crazy Love* that I have repeated hundreds of times since then. "Our greatest fear," says pastor Tim Kizziar, "should not be of failure but of succeeding at things in life that don't really matter."[1]

Isn't this so? Wouldn't it be a terrible waste of this one life to spend it chasing after things that don't matter? Even if we were victorious in accumulating all the world has to offer, would any of us consider our life a success if our things proved to be worthless?

I think that's what Jesus meant when He warned us, "What good is it for someone to gain the whole world, yet forfeit their soul?" (Mark 8:36).

What if we're defining success in the wrong way and have fallen into a trap?

What if all that the world offers is not the best good we can pursue?

As you live out Jesus's teachings on money and possessions, pay attention to how His invitation begins to open your mind to a whole new understanding of success. A life well lived may be something quite different than you have been assuming or the world has been proclaiming. You may already be on your way to questioning the common portrayal of success—I hope you are. Minimalism can help you make the full transition to a new vision of achievement as well as settle on the best life choices for you and your family.

One way to test where you are in the journey from an old view of success to a new one is to ask yourself whom you look up to.

Two Visitors

Imagine you are on your church's welcome team. On Sundays you keep an eye out for visitors, making yourself available to say a friendly word and help newcomers find a seat.

One Sunday, two unrelated men walk through the doors of the church. The first man is someone you've heard of and recognize. This man is well put together, wears a fitted suit, drove up in a nice car, lives in that "big house on the side of the hill," and is known around town for owning a lot of property and being a successful, if not hard-nosed, businessman. Today, for whatever reason, he has decided to come to church. He seems pleasant enough and enters with a smile and a confident air, shoulders back.

The second man, who walks through a different door at almost the same time, looks much different, to say the least. His clothes aren't neat or well fitting—*shabby* might be a better word to describe how he looks. He clearly struggles to make ends meet financially. He shuffles in, downtrodden, looking at the floor, appearing nervous to make eye contact. He presents quite a contrast to the well-known man in the community walking in at the same time.

You stand alone as the only greeter in your church lobby. Who gets your attention first? Which of those two men gets your first handshake and invitation to try out the church's coffee shop?

Maybe this question is easier to answer if you're not the one making the decision. So, let's change it slightly. Which of these two men do you think would get the most attention from the people in your church lobby?

I think it's safe to say that most of us would decide to approach the well-dressed businessman first. And it says volumes about the kinds of people we gravitate toward, admire, and want to be like.

Seeing Through the Illusion

If the scenario I just described sounds familiar, that's because it's found in a New Testament story. Jesus's half-brother James encourages us to look at success with a different lens than the one the world uses:

> Suppose a man comes into your meeting wearing a gold ring and fine clothes, and a poor man in filthy old clothes also comes in. If you show special attention to the man wearing fine clothes and say, "Here's a good seat for you," but say to the poor man, "You stand there" or "Sit on the floor by my feet," have you not discriminated among yourselves and become judges with evil thoughts? (James 2:2–4)

Not only is such behavior biased, but James takes it a step further and calls it "evil" to judge or show favoritism to the rich. This behavior may be evil for a number of reasons, but on some level, it reveals that people's value system has become inverted from the kingdom of God's. As James continues to explain, his readers may admire wealth so much that they begin looking down on those most deserving of their admiration and admiring those who least deserve it.

This is strong but important language.

Notice how James calls the church to define success differently than we are accustomed:

> Has not God chosen those who are poor in the eyes of the world to be rich in faith and to inherit the kingdom he promised those who love him? But you have dishonored the poor. Is it not the rich who are exploiting you? Are they not the ones who are dragging you into court? Are they not the ones who are blaspheming the noble name of him to whom you belong? (verses 5–7)

How much are we like the people James accuses of having warped priorities? Probably more than we'd like to admit. Even in today's church, we are quick to celebrate those who live in large homes, drive nice cars, and walk through the doors with expensive clothes and jewelry. Often we show them favoritism without knowing much about them or how they acquired their money.

Should we really be admiring and wanting to be like people who spend their money on cars and homes and clothes and jewelry to an excessive extent? Aren't there better uses of God-given resources? Aren't there better goals to aim for, finer values to serve as our compass? Isn't the man or woman who holds this world with a loose grip more admirable than the one who clings to it tightly?

We live in a world where achievement is often measured by wealth and possessions, along with fame. Everywhere we look, and in every message we hear from the surrounding culture, we're told to define success in terms of worldly gain. Minimalism makes us step back and ask, *Is this really what success is?* It causes us to recognize the illusion and to look at life through a new, Christ-centered lens. When we adopt a minimalist approach to life, it ushers in newfound opportunity to define success the way God does.

But wait! you might object. *Isn't wealth a sign of God's blessing? Isn't it a* good *thing, not a danger?*

Let's see.

A Theology of Blessing

In the Old Testament, it is true that God often showed His favor to people through material blessing. He gave great riches to Job—twice! In the context of blessing Abraham, God promised that this patriarch's descendants would inherit a great extent of land. Abraham's herds grew and grew, and so did his grandson Jacob's. David became rich enough to build himself a palace and fund the building of the temple. And most famously of all, King Solomon took his inheritance from David and built on it to become the richest king of his day (2 Chronicles 9:22).

So, isn't it true that God shows His favor to those who are the most faithful by blessing them with material wealth? Not at all. In fact, that type of thinking can be very dangerous.

In the Old Testament era, God was building a literal, physical kingdom—His nation of Israel. But in New Testament times, God initiated something different. Starting with those great minimalists John the Baptist and Jesus, God began building a spiritual kingdom (John 18:36).

This is important to understand. While building a physical nation on earth, God's blessing for obedience and faithfulness was the expanse of that physical kingdom. It makes sense that faithfulness in that kingdom resulted in material gain. But the growth of His spiritual kingdom in both the world and our lives looks very different. In a spiritual kingdom (which is much better, by the way), blessing looks like love and peace, personal change and spiritual growth, and the voice of the Holy Spirit available and followed in our lives. And sometimes material possessions stand in the way of that spiritual growth.

Now, don't misinterpret what I'm saying. I'm not contending that it is impossible for a rich person to live a godly life. There are examples in Scripture. And I personally know many wealthy individuals who honor God with their lives and resources. Jesus Himself declared it possible (Luke 18:27).

Nor am I saying that making or possessing money is always bad or that somehow poverty in itself equates with godliness. This would be the counter-mistake.

I'm just saying that, for us, God's greatest blessings are spiritual in nature. And it's best to think of having wealth not so much as God giving a blessing to spend on ourselves but as Him assigning us a responsibility to use it for His kingdom first and foremost. That is what success looks like in God's economy.

Gaining Friends

Jesus told a curious parable about a manager who was about to get fired for misusing his master's money (Luke 16:1–15). This manager came up with a bold plan to protect himself. He gave discounts to the master's creditors, with the implication that they would help him out later, when he was broke and out of a job.

To be honest, for a long time this parable had me scratching my head trying to figure out the point of it. The manager appears more dishonest than shrewd. But sometime after I found minimalism, the important truth behind this parable clicked for me.

Of course Jesus was *not* saying we should cheat our employers. But in another sense, the manager had done something smart.

Jesus drew this conclusion for His followers: "I tell you, use worldly wealth to gain friends for yourselves, so that when it is gone, you will be welcomed into eternal dwellings" (verse 9). In other words, while we are in this world, we are to use our money to connect with people, help others, and advance the kingdom of God, and then we will receive eternal rewards for it.

Those who are faithful to God with their blessings will be given more responsibility. As Jesus said, "Whoever can be trusted with very little can also be trusted with much, and whoever is dishonest with very little will also be dishonest with much. So if you have not been trustworthy in handling worldly wealth, who will trust you with true riches?" (verses 10–11). We are entrusted with more wealth not to build our own personal kingdoms on earth but to invest in God's kingdom.

Jesus told this parable to the Pharisees, who, like too many Christians today, thought they could combine being highly religious with being in love with money. It was to them that Jesus said, "No one can serve two masters. Either you will hate the one and love the other, or you will be devoted to the one and despise the other. You cannot serve both God and money" (verse 13).

We have admitted to ourselves that we tend to admire the rich. Well, Jesus is blunt about that attitude: "What people value highly is detestable in God's sight" (verse 15).

The sooner we let minimalism inspire a radical mental transformation about what success means, the better.

Don't Wait

During my days as a pastor, I once had the sad task of counseling a couple from our church whose teenage daughter had died suddenly in a car accident. Of course the parents were heartbroken by this unanticipated tragedy. They both looked haggard and long faced when I met with them. The wife's eyes were red from crying. What struck me most, though, was the change in the husband.

Prior to this meeting, the man had intimidated me. He was always *so* driven, *so* self-assured, *so* plainly successful (in the worldly sense). He had risen to a place of great importance in his company, and his family was well cared for financially. As a result, he radiated pride and a sense of security. When he walked into a room, everyone wanted to shake his hand and be noticed by him. His attitude seemed to say that he had it all.

And then he lost his daughter.

Now he was like a different person. His countenance had changed dramatically, from one of boldness and confidence to one of devastation and distress. From a position of pride, he had become humble. Instead of feeling sure of himself, he was searching for answers and reconsidering his whole approach to life.

With tears in his eyes, he told me, "I didn't even get to see her that day because I chose to work late. I was so busy at the office that I missed my opportunity to say goodbye when she left the house, and now it's too late."

Certainly this man was not responsible for the car accident that took his daughter's life. And I hope by now he has learned not to make too much of failing to say goodbye to his daughter.

But make no mistake, this was one of those moments that we all face from time to time that cause us to pause and reflect on what really matters in the long run. Even if we are unusually fortunate in this life, it is inevitable that we will *all* reach the end of our time on earth and be forced to discover whether we ran toward the correct finish line. James adds to his commentary on pursuing worldly gain this way: "The rich will fade away even while they go about their business" (1:11).

It is easy to chase the world, as this bereaved father had done (and many of us do), especially when you experience some success in taking hold of it. But there is incredible opportunity for those who resist the temptation. We shouldn't wait until tragedy has struck or we have come to the end of our lives to reconsider our priorities.

I'm about to tell you how you can do that.

The Two Questions You Need to Find Real Success

Our immeasurably creative God has a great diversity of plans for us, but I believe success will always involve building His kingdom, not ours. And with that perspective in mind, I have identified two questions that I think all believers can effectually ask themselves to reorient toward real success.

1. **Am I becoming more like Jesus?**

   We often like to quote Romans 8:28: "We know that in all things God works for the good of those who love him, who have been called according to his purpose." But what is "the good" that all things work together for? We find it in the context of this verse. "The good" that God desires to bring about in our lives is that we would be more and more conformed to the image of Christ. The very next verse says it clearly: "For those God foreknew he also predestined *to be conformed to the image of his Son*" (verse 29, emphasis added).

What a beautiful promise! God's desire for our lives—more than that, the very work He is doing—is to lovingly mold us to look more like the Son He loves.

So, are you becoming more like Jesus in love, in relationships, in word, and in actions? Do you prioritize conversation with the heavenly Father as He did? Do you speak the truth as boldly? Do you go to the needy as readily? Do you have a similar humility? Do you hold the world as loosely? Or have you given in to the temptation that surrounds you to be conformed to this world instead?

Rather than admiring the rich and hoping to be like them, let's keep our eyes fixed on Jesus and make Him our model at all times.

Here's a rule of thumb: If you don't know whether you are becoming more like Jesus, then you probably aren't. Why? Because from everything I can tell, looking like Jesus is hard work. It requires focus. Sometimes it is messy. It is difficult, it is painful at times, and it requires discipline and intentionality.

But a life undistracted by too much of the world's toys and trappings is a life where you can work through all this. Minimalism makes it easier to make real progress in Christlikeness.

If you are becoming more like Jesus, your life is a success no matter what it looks like from the outside or how it compares to the life you expected. This is God's great design for our lives—to grant us the privilege of beginning to look like His beloved Son.

2. **Am I doing the work God has chosen for me?**

   There's another popular Bible passage we like to quote because of its clarity about the *basis* of our salvation: "It is by grace you have been saved, through faith—and this is not from yourselves, it is the gift of God—not by works, so that no one can boast" (Ephesians 2:8–9). Yet too often, we stop reading after these verses and do not notice that this passage also describes the *purpose or goal* of our salvation: "For we are God's handiwork, created in Christ Jesus to do good works, which God prepared in advance for us to do" (verse 10). God has saved us—not just for the sake of our souls but also for the good works He has prepared for each of us to accomplish for His kingdom.

   This is success. Not that we would live in larger houses, eat at fancier restaurants, go on more extravagant vacations, have bigger bank account balances, or be able to retire earlier in life. Only a fool measures achievement in those terms. Success happens when I take all that God has given me, in the place where He has put me, and accomplish what He has called me to do.

   Sometimes that means we change one person's life. Sometimes it means we change a hundred or a thousand people's lives, or more. If it's the impact God wants us to have, it is enough and we will receive an eternal reward.

All of us should be moving toward the goal of Christlikeness. But our designated "good works" are beautifully diverse, individual to us, and fitted to who God made us to be.

Success is being in tune with God to be and do what He calls us to. We should ask ourselves the questions *Am I becoming more like Jesus?* and *Am I doing the work God has chosen for me?* not just once but periodically throughout our lives. They will help us keep recalibrating according to God's measures of success.

A Holiday at the Sea

One of the most influential thoughts during my early journey into minimalism came from this quote by C. S. Lewis: "It would seem that Our Lord finds our desires not too strong, but too weak. We are half-hearted creatures, fooling about with drink and sex and ambition when infinite joy is offered us, like an ignorant child who wants to go on making mud pies in a slum because he cannot imagine what is meant by the offer of a holiday at the sea. We are far too easily pleased."[2]

In the context of uncluttered faith, these words reveal an important truth about how many of us live. We've been chasing the mud pies of materialism and worldly success, when God is offering us infinite joy and infinite purpose.

Minimalism is the countercultural step we need to take to wake from our slumber and break free from the world's illusions. Putting into practice Jesus's teachings on money and possessions helps us see, in a brand-new way, that our lives are too valuable to waste chasing material possessions. There is an infinitely greater definition of success we can discover.

Let go of the mud pies, start owning less, and you'll find the temptation to define success in worldly terms begin to vanish. The "holiday at the sea" of kingdom participation is so much greater.

12

A Purpose Beyond the Paycheck

One evening I sat outside around a fire with two prosperous entrepreneurs, both wonderful human beings and followers of Jesus. It was our first opportunity to really get to know one another. As they began asking me questions about my work, the conversation steered toward minimalism. I shared about not just the work I do around the topic but also the profound positive impact minimalism has had on my family.

My friends were intrigued but skeptical. They could understand the connection between clutter and distraction and even commented on how clean they like to keep their garages. But as we began to press deeper into the implications, the notion that one could maintain ambition without pursuing larger houses in nicer neighborhoods, more expensive cars, financial success, and an abundance of material possessions for one's family seemed foreign to them.

One of the men remarked, "I think I'm too entrepreneurial. That's just my heart. And my drive for nicer stuff is what keeps me motivated, which is a good thing for my business. I don't think the minimalist lifestyle is for me. It would kill my motivation for succeeding in business."

I thought, *Well, I'm an entrepreneur, too, you know.* But my audible response was this: "I'm not suggesting we lose ambition. I'm suggesting we can find greater ambition by redirecting it toward more meaningful pursuits than the accumulation of material possessions."

Minimalism lowers the amount of money we require to maintain a chosen standard of living, removing the need to earn ever-increasing sums. We begin to see that the motivation for our work doesn't have to be the numbers on our paychecks. We can direct our passions at work and in our careers toward something more lasting and more fulfilling. Our entire motivation for this important area of life can change. And when it does, the world, God's kingdom, our families, and our own selves will begin to change for the better.

Did you know that in the course of a lifetime we each spend about ninety thousand hours at work? That's one-third of our lives on this earth![1] So, it's important that we get this part of our lives right.

I believe that most of us Christians understand that honoring God ought to be our objective for our work, same as for every other part of life (1 Corinthians 10:31). It's just that in our careers we tend to get caught up in exactly the same frantic moneymaking endeavors that everyone else does. We need something to break us out of this cycle, because God invites us to something better.

Minimalism makes it easier to focus on God's glory rather than our paychecks as the chief goal of our work. And let me assure you, there's something truly beautiful in how that switch of perspectives transforms our jobs and our lives.

Choose Your Boss

We should already know better than to get caught up in the "I'm in it for the paycheck" attitude, because two thousand years ago the apostle Paul gave us a better way of thinking about work. He said it this way: "Whatever you do, work at it with all your heart, as working for the Lord, not for human masters" (Colossians 3:23).

If you're like me, you'd *like* to do your work as unto the Lord. But that can seem almost impossible if we're looking at work as the means through which we make the money to buy all the stuff we want and live the comfortable lives the world offers us.

As we see the value of a minimalist lifestyle, however, our thoughts and motivation for work begin to change. For one thing, minimalism significantly alters how much money we need to live. Work doesn't have to be about making more if it is already providing enough. Our time, talents, expertise, and skills in our work can be used for God's glory rather than trying to build our own kingdoms and castles.

If I am not a minimalist, I see my paycheck as the means through which I can afford that bigger house or cooler truck or second house on the lake. The only limiting factor on how much money I can spend on stuff is how much money I have. But deciding to live a minimalist life creates positive limitations. Sure, I have to take time to figure out what I need, and those needs might change with the seasons of life. But the parameters are basically set at "I want to own just what I need to own."

And as soon as the boundaries are set, I get to ask a brand-new-to-me question: "What am I going to do with my income since I don't need it to buy more stuff?" Again, all the worldly temptations still exist: I can hoard it; I can go on luxurious vacations; and so on. Getting as much as possible can still be my motivation. But if God is directing my steps and I am open in a new way to seeing that I don't need as much as I can get for myself, I can begin to see my work in a new way. I can bill for less. I can volunteer my talents more. I can help someone else get ahead. I can choose to charge the single mother less than I would have before. God is still meeting my needs—but my flexibility and approach have changed because I've set a limitation.

An Unbeatable Reward Offer

I've said it before: There's always a promise on the other side of every biblical command. Obedience is for our own good. And that is clearly the case with working for the Lord.

Here is the Colossians 3:23–24 passage in full: "Whatever you do, work at it with all your heart, as working for the Lord, not for human masters, *since you know that you will receive an inheritance from the Lord as a reward.* It is the Lord Christ you are serving" (emphasis added).

Think about that for a moment. The inheritance God offers us isn't something that will perish, spoil, or fade. It is an eternal inheritance, meaning it will last *forever.* It's perfect. And that's something this world can never offer.

Yes, you can work for yourself, your paycheck, and your own glory—but those rewards won't last. Or you can work for God's glory, His kingdom, and His purposes, knowing that your effort is never wasted when it's done for Him.

Receiving inheritances from the Lord as rewards for our work is infinitely better than any number of zeros at the ends of our paychecks or worldly status our careers might provide. Don't you love the idea of seeing your work and career as something you do in the Lord's service rather than for your boss or selfish pursuits?

This perspective changes everything. Suddenly, even the most mundane daily tasks—answering emails, doing the laundry, sitting in a meeting, or running errands—can be acts of worship, worked on and accomplished as if the Lord Himself had asked us to do them.

And when we do them with all our hearts, as unto the Lord, they carry eternal significance. This is the ultimate paycheck for the work you do each day. Can you imagine? Being rewarded by God Himself for the eight or so hours a day we each put in at work?

So right now, think about your work. Is it something you are doing with all your heart, motivated by love, selflessness, joy, and hope—not for fleeting recognition or for the stuff it enables you to buy but for the glory of God? If so, I'm happy for you, because the reward God promises is worth it. But if not, then becoming minimalist offers you a potentially life-changing opportunity to rethink your work life.

The Root of Evil Is the Fruit of Labor

I don't want to imply that income is not relevant in our work. The Bible makes it clear in 1 Timothy that "anyone who does not provide for their relatives, and especially for their own household, has denied the faith and is worse than an unbeliever" (5:8). To provide for one's family as is commanded, one has to earn a living.

As we work, God will provide financially for our needs. Sadly, though, many of us have long moved beyond contentment with God providing our needs into wanting constant upgrades for our lives in this world. And when this becomes normalized, there is never an end to the amount of money we want to make from our work.

I'm not contending that we do our work for free or let ourselves be exploited by those who are motivated entirely by the bottom line. Equally, I'm not saying we should purposely limit our earning potential. If our priorities are correct—God's glory being the first motivation for our work—then it's okay if our work produces a large income. In fact, Christians should make the best employees (at least in terms of their morality and work ethic), and that should eventually result in suitable reward.

I have known many people who are incredibly gifted by God with sharp business minds. My two friends around the firepit stand as proof. Likewise, if God has created you with talents and treasures to succeed in business, keep on succeeding! Making God our first priority at work doesn't mean we forfeit our gifts and skills.

For those with business-oriented gifts, my hope is that you are both doing your best work for the glory of God, motivated by your love for Him, *and* giving away as much as possible to support Christ's Great Commission. Because that is probably the exact role God has prepared for you to fulfill—and there are so many wonderful Christian ministries and organizations desperately needing your giftedness and gifts.

Actually, that's a good goal for all of us. However much you are earning in your work, do the best you can, work fully for the sake of God's kingdom rather than your own, provide for your needs, and give the rest away.

John Wesley preached, "No more sloth! Whatsoever your hand findeth to do, do it with your might! No more waste! Cut off every expense which fashion, caprice, or flesh and blood demand! No more covetousness! But employ whatever God has entrusted you with, in doing good, all possible good, in every possible kind and degree to the household of faith, to all men!"[2]

Minimalism provides the pathway to choose God's kingdom rather than our own kingdoms as the goal of our work.

Minister Mom

Working for the Lord does not necessarily mean having a paid ministry position. In fact, it might mean not having a paid position at all. A stay-at-home parent, for example, works just as hard for their family's well-being as their externally employed spouse. And a retired individual can be working in valuable volunteer service even if not paid.

A minister, an accountant, a CEO, and a grocery store cashier can all (and are all commanded to) do their work as unto the Lord and for the glory of God. And for all of them, minimalism may be the missing element that enables them to maximize the kingdom potential of their work.

Amy Hetzer of San Diego is a mother of five, including two with severe special needs (a son with a rare chromosome deletion and a daughter with cerebral palsy). For her, taking care of these kids is her job. And after a while she reached a point of feeling overwhelmed with the responsibility for care placed on her. Simplifying her life through minimalism brought her back to the basics that helped her find joy and success in her job again.

"I had to remember God gave me these children," said Amy, "and what mattered were His expectations of me. I had let my own unrealistic demands and outside social media idealism set the bar so high. I began to whittle down to what truly mattered."

She asked herself about her kids with special needs, *Are they safe? Do they have a clean home? Are their basic needs being met?*

"As I filtered through this important part of my life, it helped me find joy again in caregiving, instead of always feeling like I was falling short. This re-energized me to attempt creative ideas for my children, but as a bonus, not an essential."

Minimalism continues to help Amy in her role as a parent and to flow into every area of her life.

Our Work for the Kingdom

If Kingdom of God Inc. and World Inc. were included in an employee satisfaction survey, there would be no comparison in the results. Working for God's kingdom is the greatest possible way to use one's time and gifts. As minimalism enables us to choose God's purposes rather than our own as the goal of our work, something incredible happens—we find deeper purpose, greater joy, and a more lasting impact in what we do each day. It's simply an amazing way to live!

Consider a few specifics of what working for the Lord and His kingdom means for our lives.

It has eternal effects.

When working for an eternal kingdom is our goal, the impact of our work doesn't have to end with our paychecks—or even the conclusion of our lives. Every day, we get to invest in something that lasts forever: lives changed, good news proclaimed, hope lifted, and a legacy established.

It is rewarded with eternal treasure.

As we've already seen, God's promise is clear: When we work for Him rather than ourselves, we receive an inheritance that cannot fade or be taken away.

It brings us greater fulfillment.

There's a reason studies repeatedly show that money doesn't bring happiness[3]—namely, because money is fleeting and temporal and cannot offer fulfillment to the same degree as God's purpose and meaning. Choosing the Lord instead of the paycheck as the goal of your work results in greater satisfaction—not just at the end of your life but also every night when you lay your head on your pillow.

It motivates us to work harder.

The wife of Joseph Alleine, a persecuted pastor from the 1600s, recalled that he was troubled if he heard smiths or other craftsmen at work at their trades before he was at work in his ministry. He would say to her, "O how this noise shames me! Does not my master deserve more than *theirs?*"[4] I have long thought of that quote since the first time I heard it in college. Doesn't our God deserve more of our effort than the idols of this world do?

Yes. And when our motivation for work becomes something as important as the glory of God, we actually become more motivated to work harder and give more of ourselves to our jobs.

It sets a better example.

People, I believe, are watching not just *how* but also *why* we work. If we do our work for selfish reasons, others leave unimpressed or even disgusted. But if we work for unselfish reasons, we set a powerful example—not only for other believers but for the world too.

It results in greater joy.

How often do we chase after things we think will make us happy, only to be left exhausted and unfulfilled? But when we do our work with the mindset of serving God, we find an unexpected joy—the joy of knowing our efforts have meaning beyond ourselves.

It helps us overcome envy.

When we align our work with the values of God's kingdom, we are free to stop measuring success by someone else's paycheck or job title. The greatest step to overcome envy is to align our lives with our values. When the goal of work becomes God's kingdom rather than ours, envy loses its grip.

It is why we were created.

As we work for the glory of God, we are fulfilling the very purposes for which we were made. Imagine living out the great purpose you were created for, every single day—at work, at home, at church. What passion and joy you could find in shifting your focus in this way!

It is something we can control.

Chasing financial success is never entirely within our hands. Market trends, competition, economic downturns, sheer luck, and even the whims of a fickle boss all play roles in determining who rises and who falls. But when the glory of God is our motivation, none of those factors determine our success. Every hour of every day, we are in control of whether we are thriving or not.

What It's All About

I've reached some pretty big career milestones and received some flattering accolades during my years of minimalism advocacy. But here's the thing: I'm not the greatest businessman, manager, leader, or writer—I know that to be true. I didn't start a blog to get famous or make a bunch of money anyway. I haven't run my business with an eye on an ever-increasing income or earning greater worldly rewards. Yet, by most accounts, I have done fairly well. Why is that?

For one thing, I credit much of the success of Becoming Minimalist to my passion for genuinely wanting to help others own less. My first desire is to serve. I think people see and appreciate that and are drawn to it. That desire also compels me to be better at what I do.

But if I stopped there, my explanation would be incomplete and misleading. Because there's an even deeper level.

After reading this chapter, perhaps you'll better understand this underlying principle of my work: My greatest purpose is not being helpful to people just to increase the bottom line. I genuinely believe I am doing my part to *advance the purposes of* God in this world *by helping people own less.* A desire to build the kingdom of God in my own particular way is the bedrock of everything I do.

I believe that as I try to be faithful, God sends the blessing. So, of course, He gets all the glory! That's just the way it should be.

But boy, what a fun thing to be a part of!

I'm so thankful that I simplified my life so I could look at my purpose in a new way and take a chance on doing work differently.

You and I may not have ninety thousand hours left to go in our careers, but we probably have quite a few. Let's make them count.

13

Less Stuff, More Giving

When I started minimizing, I was discontented with my finances. Can you relate?

I bet most of you can. Around 80 percent of Americans report some level of stress around their finances.[1] Nearly as many are living paycheck to paycheck, like the Becker family was before minimalism came into our lives.[2]

But here's the thing: I was discontented not just with how much money I was spending but also with whom I was spending my money on.

I grew up in church, and I knew what God says about taking care of widows and orphans. I knew full well He calls us to live a countercultural life of generosity toward the poor and the needy. It sure seems, when you read His words, that He is calling us to give more than 10 percent of what we take in. My wife and I were just never able to get there. It seemed that no matter how much we wanted to, we could never go beyond the mere tithe. Or to put it another way, we were always spending 90 percent of our money on ourselves.

One of the great joys I found after becoming a minimalist was finally being able to give like I wanted. We had more money for our own uses, and at the same time, we could give more money to our church and an array of ministries and good causes.

If you have a yearning in your heart to be more generous with your finances, minimalism may be just what you need to make that possible. It is the often-neglected pathway to the generous life God calls us to live.

In fact, I would say that *only* when we live out Christ's teachings on possessions can we discover the margin to live out His teachings on generosity. Minimalism allows us to become generous in more ways and to a greater degree than we ever thought possible. The personal satisfaction in that, as well as the potential it creates for eternal impact, is awesome to think about.

This perspective on possessions and generosity is one that we Christians have largely lost—but that we *can* recover.

Like the Early Church

One Wednesday night, I spoke at a local church on the spiritual discipline of simplicity. I shared my journey into minimalism and the life-changing benefits of owning less. When we did a Q&A afterward, many of the usual questions emerged about how to apply these principles in specific circumstances. Then one woman stood up toward the end with a question I had never heard in more than fifteen years of having this conversation.

She asked, "If every person here took this very seriously, practiced minimalism, and applied this mentality to their homes and time and family for a year, what change do you believe would occur in our church?"

I paused to think because it was such a deep and rich question. After a few moments, I gave an answer that I believe came from God. It was true then, and it is true today. I responded, "If we all began to live out these principles of intentionally owning less, I believe the church today would begin to look more like the early church did."

This is what I was getting at: If we adopt minimalism, we're not adding something trendy, contrary, or alien to our faith. We're in fact getting closer to the Christian faith as it was originally designed and modeled.

Remember Acts 2:44–45: "All the believers were together and had everything in common. They sold property and possessions to give to anyone who had need." I don't know how literally we should take that (they had *everything* in common?), but this much is certain: During the birth of the church, simplicity and generosity didn't seem optional or debatable to the new believers—they were distinct characteristics of the community. They took to heart Jesus's teachings on money and possessions, and the church flourished because of it.

We can be sure this was true, because the same point is made again a little later in the book of Acts: "All the believers were one in heart and mind. No one claimed that any of their possessions was their own, but they shared everything they had. . . . And God's grace was so powerfully at work in them all that there were no needy persons among them. For from time to time those who owned land or houses sold them, brought the money from the sales and put it at the apostles' feet, and it was distributed to anyone who had need" (4:32–35).

I find it interesting that this generosity happened during a time of persecution for the early Christians. Despite that hardship—or maybe because of it—they were willing to give and to share. So, is it possible that our affluence and comfort make it harder for us to be generous? I think so.

Allow me to speculate a little further.

I also find it interesting that right after this, Luke (the author of Acts) records the first sin with major ramifications to happen in the new church: Ananias and Sapphira withholding some of their money and lying about it to the apostles (5:1–11). Coming after the portrayal of an almost idyllic Christian community, this story almost reminds me of the first sin in the Garden of Eden. And what does it involve? Lying about their generosity.

An overattachment to wealth may be the great American sin of our day, as I have characterized it, but the temptation to clutch one's possessions rather than be openhanded in faith is clearly a perpetual sin. Jesus resisted the temptation to receive "all the kingdoms of the world and their splendor" by worshipping the devil (Matthew 4:8). Yet we cave in spiritually when it's just a matter of desiring a bunch of unnecessary household goods. We may try to excuse ourselves on the basis that it's too hard to give more or that everybody is being selfish with their money, so why shouldn't we?

I think we'd better take this matter of generosity very seriously. And as always, we'll find that the call to sacrifice our financial resources comes with a reward that far exceeds any temporary cost to ourselves.

Converting Good Intentions

Writing to a group of Christians two thousand years ago, the apostle John posed a question: "If anyone has material possessions and sees a brother or sister in need but has no pity on them, how can the love of God be in that person?" (1 John 3:17). I think that question is still valid.

If we're not moved by compassion when presented with others' needs, if we always find a reason *not* to share whatever money or goods we possess, perhaps we should ask ourselves whether God's love dwells in our hearts. After all, God gave the most precious thing He had—His one and only Son—to meet our need for redemption. Giving, then, can be a critical gauge for whether our hearts are aligned with God's heart.

Yet I believe most people reading this book are *not* pitiless or loveless. You are likely part of the large group of Christians who are already giving to help others and only wish they could give more. You don't want to be greedy; you just can't seem to find the margin to give more. Something's hindering you. Your inadequate generosity is probably a source of frustration or even discontent or guilt for you, as mine was for me.

Isn't it curious that in one of the wealthiest nations ever to exist, Christians struggle to give? The early church gave freely during a time of persecution and oppression, yet we find it difficult. According to one study, only 10 percent of American evangelicals tithe (that is, give 10 percent to their church), and half gave less than $250 per year to church and charity combined.[3] Now, Christians tend to give about 40 percent more to charity than non-Christians, so there's some cause for celebration.[4] Still, it's clear that we could do much better. There is plenty of money in the world to fund all the amazing work God wants to accomplish through His people; we just need to loosen our grips and share it.

If you want to give more, pay close attention to the next verse John wrote: "Dear children, let us not love with words or speech but with actions and in truth" (verse 18). Our instinct to be more generous is a good one. But good intentions aren't love. And neither is speech. We must find a way to get past our mere good intentions and convert them to action, actually giving more.

How? Minimalism provides the means. Owning less creates the missing margin in our finances and makes it possible for us to give more. It also weakens our emotional attachments to our money, making it easier to give what we can.

Jesus's words "It is more blessed to give than to receive" (Acts 20:35) have entered common culture as a cliché, but that doesn't make them any less true. Far from being boring (as many people view it), minimalism is thrilling, in part because it enables us to pursue our passions and be a part of the great works God is doing in our day. With open hearts of compassion for the needs around us, we can open our hands and share what God has shared with us.

A blessed life indeed. Made possible for you—if you're willing—by minimalism.

The Money You Save

Let's do a reality check. Does becoming a minimalist *really* put more money in your pocket—money that you can then give to the Lord's work and good causes? Yes, it does. I'm going to prove it to you with numbers.

Some of the financial margin comes from selling stuff you're getting rid of. You can be like the early Christians who liquidated their unneeded possessions for cash to give away to people who needed it more.

When my friend Bob Lotich and his wife, Linda, minimized their home, Bob—a personal finance educator—kept track of what they made by selling off things. (Apparently he loves spreadsheets more than the rest of us.) Listing old books, a mountain bike, the high chair their child no longer needed, and much more on three online reselling sites, the Lotichs made

$2,145. Bob figures he spent at most ten hours doing these sales, so he made more than $200 per hour on it. Not bad.[5]

Obviously, the money you make on unwanted objects depends on what you've got and how you go about selling them. The money you recoup may be less or more than the Lotichs made.

In any case, for nearly everyone, selling unwanted items is *not* the main way that minimalism makes cash available. The best way to make money from your clutter is to not buy it in the first place! Most of our financial gain comes from the money we save going forward by spending less and owning less.

I decided to do some back-of-the-envelope type of calculations to try to figure out how minimalism can contribute to financial savings. And according to my math, the average American family can free up almost $25,000 per year through minimalism. To arrive at that number, I looked at nine spending categories we can lower through owning and buying fewer things.

1. **Nonessentials**

   According to one study, the average American spends $1,002 per month on nonessential items.[6] Does becoming minimalist mean you'll eliminate all nonessential purchases? Certainly not. (In fact, I'm writing this chapter while sitting in a coffee shop waiting for a friend to arrive. My caramel macchiato isn't exactly an essential.) But let's assume, for the purposes of this calculation, that you can save $12,000 a year by removing many of your nonessential purchases.

2. **Housing**

   Nationwide, as of early 2025, the national average monthly mortgage payment is $2,200.[7] Saving 25 percent each month by downsizing could result in $6,600 in annual savings. But that seems too high of a number to plug into our equation. So, let's compare rent rather than mortgage.

The average rent difference between two-bedroom and three-bedroom apartments in the United States is $480 per month, or $5,760 per year, as reported by Apartments.com.[8] So, I'll use that number. Let's say you can save $5,760 a year by moving into a smaller home.

3. **Utility bills**

   According to This Old House, the average monthly residential utility bill is around $590.[9] By minimizing your space, you could reduce this cost by another 25 percent, saving you around $1,770 a year.

4. **Home maintenance and repair costs**

   Bankrate estimates that U.S. households will spend an average of $8,800 on home maintenance in 2025.[10] A conservative estimate might be a 10 percent savings on maintenance and repair costs, which averages to about $880 a year.

5. **Homeowners insurance**

   The average homeowner's insurance cost in the United States, as of September 2025, is "hovering around $3,000 per year."[11] Continuing with the cost savings of living in a smaller home, let's assume you can save 20 percent of that amount, or $600 each year.

6. **Clothing**

   The average American household spends about $2,041 on apparel every year.[12] With a minimalist approach, you can easily cut this in half by only replacing worn-out clothing rather than expanding your wardrobe, saving around $1,000 per year.

7. **Food**

According to some estimates, the average American family of four wastes about $1,600 worth of food each year.[13] Becoming more intentional with your meals and grocery shopping, you could likely cut that down by 25 percent, saving $400 per year.

8. **Gifts**

The average American family spends more than $2,000 per year on gifts and holiday spending.[14] By agreeing with friends and family to limit gift giving to necessary items or experiences, let's assume you can save $500 per year.

9. **Debt repayment**

In the first half of 2025, the average credit card balance was $6,473.[15] Since the average interest rate (as of this writing) is around 21 percent, those credit card users will each spend $1,359 per year in interest alone. By adopting minimalism and using the newfound savings to pay down debt, you'll eventually get to a point where you can save that expense.

Let's not assume you'll get out of credit card debt the first year you embrace minimalism, so I'll plug in $1,200 per year in savings.

Total potential savings

Adding these up, the potential annual savings of becoming a minimalist could be around $24,110.

Again, the actual number for you might be more or less, depending on your personal circumstances. But my estimate gives you an idea of how minimalism can have a significant, positive impact on your financial situation.

And let's not forget the point of it all: This is money you can redirect from unnecessary expenses to causes that help build God's kingdom and earn you heavenly reward.

Cheerful Giver

I hope my rudimentary calculations have convinced you that those who minimize should start seeing a savings. The crucial question is, what will *you* do with *your* newly available resources?

I know a lot of people who spend their extra cash on things like traveling and leisure activities. There may be nothing wrong with these things, at least in moderation. Sometimes, though, I look at my fellow minimalists and think they have traded the *worse* for the *better* yet still have fallen short of the *best*.

We Christians should view saving money by minimizing not just as a way to make our own lives more pleasant but also as a chance to invest in the kingdom of God and make life better for others.

Generosity doesn't just happen, even if we have more money on hand. There's always something else to spend our money on—the evil one will make sure we're *very* aware of that. In addition to a release of money through simplifying, there must also be a choice—an act of the will—to develop new habits of giving generously.

Thankfully, minimalism does more than just save us money and enable us to give. It also helps weaken our hearts' attachment to money, making it easier for us to be generous. When we understand that we really don't need to spend as much money on ourselves as we thought and we begin to redefine what success looks like, we will see greater potential for our money, viewing it as a resource we can use in different ways. Suddenly we're no longer feeling bad about not giving away more; we're ready—and excited—to take our generosity to a new level!

Maybe you're just starting to see some financial benefits from minimalism and you don't have a lot of extra money to give yet, although you're expecting more later. My advice in that case? Don't wait. Start with what you've got.

A little can mean a lot.

The Power of Small Gifts

On Tuesday of Jesus's final week of earthly life, He sat down in the court of the temple where the offering boxes were kept—thirteen trumpet-shaped receptacles. People were lined up to give their offerings. Many rich people threw in lots of coinage, which must have made a loud noise and gained a lot of approving attention from those watching. But then another person approached that only Jesus took notice of.

"A poor widow came and put in two very small copper coins, worth only a few cents" (Mark 12:42).

Each of her coins was equal to one-sixty-fourth of a denarius. A denarius was the typical wage for a day's labor at that time.[16] So, based on Arizona's current minimum wage of $14.70, each coin was worth perhaps around $1.84 in our currency.

Bible historians say it's probable that this woman was getting one coin each day from the temple's benevolence fund for the poor, just so she could (barely) survive. She didn't *have* to give this offering; she *wanted* to. And it's notable that because she had two coins, she could easily have kept one of them. Instead, she gave both.

According to Peter's memory of this day (as told to Mark), Jesus called over all His disciples. There was something He wanted them (and all of us) to learn. Jesus said, "Truly I tell you, this poor widow has put more into the treasury than all the others. They all gave out of their wealth; but she, out of her poverty, put in everything—all she had to live on" (verses 43–44).

The word translated "everything" literally means her "source of life." This dear woman did not put in the money she was going to use to buy a latte at Starbucks or a third car so her daughter had something to drive to school. This was the only money she had left to buy her food for the day.

She trusted in God entirely for her life, and she was so moved by love for Him that she gave all her money. What an example for us! Just two small coins is all she had to give, but the Lord wanted her story told for thousands of years—to serve as an example for all of us. And here we are, still talking about her.

Sources of Hope

Sometimes people ask me what I'm proud of with The Hope Effect, the nonprofit we started in 2015 to change how the world cares for orphans. They expect me to say something related to the kids we've helped. And of course that's what it's all about. But sometimes I choose to mention an aspect they wouldn't expect:

"I'm proud that we celebrate small gifts equally with large ones."

We are an organization dependent on donor contributions.

Yet inspired by this story of the poor widow and her gift of two coins, we decided from the nonprofit's founding that we would seek to honor those whom God lifts up as examples. So, we don't just approach wealthy donors for large gifts; we also spend time and energy reaching out to people with less means who still want to give what they can. Every gift matters.

Recently, I almost felt as if I were witnessing the gospel story being reenacted in the current day.

On Giving Tuesday of 2024, The Hope Effect received a donation check in the mail for twenty-five dollars from an older woman named Mildred. In the letter accompanying this check, Mildred thanked me for inspiring the minimalist lifestyle she now lives. She said it helped make giving a possibility for her.

And then she wrote these words: "My husband recently passed away, and so my financial resources have to be managed, since I am living on much less now. Still, God does provide for me each and every day, for which I am grateful to my heavenly Father!"

To me, Mildred's gift felt as significant as any of the five-figure donations that arrived that day. So, immediately upon receiving her letter, I phoned her.

As soon as she overcame the shock of someone calling to thank her for a twenty-five-dollar gift, she told me something remarkable. "I want you to know I found minimalism through you last year, and I can see now that God was preparing me. At the time, I had no idea God would take my husband home earlier this year. But I can see now that He was preparing me so that I could survive alone and without his income. I don't have much, but I no longer need much. Thank you."

In God's economy, the smallest gifts, given out of sacrifice, have the greatest return.

If you're at a place where you're disappointed in the amount you can give to the Lord's work—perhaps because you're still in the process of simplifying your lifestyle and haven't yet maximized your giving potential—go ahead and give it anyway, expecting God to do extraordinary things with it.

Generosity's Rebound

God *will* do great things with whatever amount you are able to give. He will also do great things *in you*.

Clearly, when we give away our unneeded stuff, extra money, and available time, we can make life better for others. Our excess can become a blessing. But in a beautiful way, our generosity is good for us too.

I can attest to the fact that generosity makes me feel better about myself and what I'm doing with my life. And I know I'm not alone. Many people who are generous report a greater sense of satisfaction and happiness.[17] Studies have even linked generosity to improved physical health.[18] Amazing!

Furthermore, I've observed that generous people have more fulfilling relationships. People always enjoy the company of a generous giver over that of a selfish hoarder. We are naturally attracted to individuals who have open hearts to share with others.

The generous also tend to value what they own. People who give away possessions hold their remaining possessions in higher esteem. Those who donate money are far less wasteful with the money left over. And people who give their time make better use of their remaining time.

In other words, generous people find meaning outside their possessions.

Although many folks wrap up their self-worth in net worth, generous people find their value in helping others. They quickly realize that their bank statements say nothing about their true value. Because of this, they have less desire for more. They have found fulfillment, meaning, worth, and relationships outside the acquisition of possessions.

Intentionally owning less opens the door to incredible blessing. Missionary J. Hudson Taylor stated in his autobiography, "The less I spent on myself and the more I gave to others, the fuller of happiness and blessing did my soul become."[19]

Taylor was experiencing exactly what Jesus promised: "Give, and it will be given to you. A good measure, pressed down, shaken together and running over, will be poured into your lap" (Luke 6:38).

"How I Am Practicing Generosity"

There's nothing like testimonials to let you know that something actually works. I asked on Facebook for people to tell me how owning less has allowed them to give more. Take special note of the diversity of the examples and the joy in the tone of these responses I received:

> When I stopped buying things just because they were a good deal, I found I had more money available to make meals for new moms, sick friends, and tired teachers in my life. —Amanda Miller, Minnesota

> We choose to live in a smallish bungalow, so we were able to pay off our mortgage early. Since then, we've been able to support several missionary families on an ongoing basis. —Donna McHardy, Canada

I never gave before, because I had little excess. But now that I've become minimalist, I give to my church, my library, and a local nonprofit. It's not much, but it's more than I used to do. —Jan Rodgers, Illinois

Minimalism allowed our family to become much more involved in our favorite ministry—Compassion International. We were able to sponsor more children, volunteer at more events, and even travel to visit some of our children and see the work of Compassion in person. —Kevin Foley, Oregon

When we decluttered our garage, we were able to let our local food bank use it for storage and packing food. They have used it for about thirteen years. Delighted to be able to use it for kingdom work, and really it was just storing stuff we didn't need. Brings me so much more joy! —Caroline Macdonald, Britain

We cut way back on our cable plan to give monthly to a missionary in Costa Rica. —Kris Korth, Illinois

Instead of purchasing more things, I am using the settlement from my head-on collision to help other people who are struggling or to support local charities. It has brought more joy than anything I could have bought from a store. —Trisha Dabbs, Georgia

A few years ago, I planned to buy a new handbag (one I didn't need). I was still pretty fresh in my minimalist journey, so I decided to wait and think about it. The next day we were able to purchase school supplies for a single-mom friend with three kids using the "bag money" I had intended to spend on myself. —Raechel Collins, South Carolina

My husband has a very well-paying job. We live in New Zealand. We were praying about how to respond to his high income as Christians, and we decided to live on the same amount of money the government gives to all over-sixty-fives here—kind of like a vow of poverty. We decided to go with that amount being "enough." We then save some money for our retirement and give the rest away. It is a decision that has led to us giving more away than previously, and to steadily giving more as his income has increased. —Heather Roberts, New Zealand

Minimalism allowed me to quit my job and fill in the needs of others. I've helped be a caregiver to people with cancer and helped a single mom who was getting out of an abusive relationship. I was able to help an older couple, without children, simplify their house. I've also been able to help two widows sell items to downsize. —Kimberly Witte Ashworth, Montana

If you're disappointed in your giving, leverage the power of minimalism to be able to give away more money, give it more creatively, and enjoy knowing that you are a part of sharing God's love with others.

14

Enough Is Enough

I love Thanksgiving dinner. It goes about the same every year, and I can picture it now: The table is covered with turkey, stuffing, mashed potatoes, corn, green beans, cranberry sauce, rolls, and gravy. We pause to pray . . . and then the meal starts. Everyone reaches, filling their plates with all sorts of wonderful food.

"Grandma needs the turkey."

"Why haven't I seen the gravy?"

"Kids, don't take any more rolls until we know there are enough for everybody."

"Who has the butter?"

It's a beautiful mad rush to fill our plates with everything we look forward to eating that day. It's loud and busy, everyone trying to get more, piling it on.

Then, at some point during the meal, everything changes. We eventually eat enough food and sit back in our chairs, satisfied. A quiet peace, maybe for the first time in the day, settles on us.

Oh, some people are still grabbing food—someone takes the last roll or a piece of dark meat, another finishes the potatoes—

but it doesn't bother us at all. Because we've had enough. It doesn't matter any longer what everyone is grabbing; we each feel satisfied.

This is what contentment feels like—when we reach a point of "enough" in our lives. Once we become content with our things and no longer desire "more," we're happy to finally stop rushing and just sit back, happy with how life is.

Let the neighbors run after the bigger houses or the newer cars. It doesn't matter—you are content and have enough.

The young guy in the office can work all the extra hours, trying to get ahead in the corporation. You have enough income and a family at home who needs their dad.

Christian physician Richard Swenson offers this definition: "The truest kind of biblical contentment is a state of feeling unencumbered. It is a state of absence of fear or anxiety about what we own or don't own. It is being unencumbered by comparisons, regardless of our neighbor or colleague or in-laws. It is being released from the perseveration of dark thoughts about entrapment or depression."[1]

Following through with Jesus's instructions about money and possessions helps us experience a deeper level of contentment than ever before.

Contentment and the Web of Goodness

Contentment involves a realization of how much we already have. It is an acknowledgment of the blessings and hand of God in our lives, regardless of our circumstances.

In a world driven by more—more money, more possessions, more status—it's easy to overlook the power of contentment and even harder to discover it. But learning to be content transforms our lives in profound ways.

I don't think I've met a single person who didn't desire contentment or at least speak of it in warm terms. Yet it remains elusive. Maybe it would be helpful to remind ourselves of the good it brings into our lives.

- Contentment shifts our focus from what we lack to what we have. It helps us appreciate God's gifts in our lives—our relationships, opportunities, and daily blessings. This gratitude reduces stress, improves our well-being, and even brings about physical health.[2]
- Contentment frees us from comparison. Instead of measuring ourselves against others, we focus on what truly matters: God's design for our lives rather than the world's design.
- Contentment doesn't mean giving up ambition. It means pursuing growth with peace. (I'll talk more about that later.)
- Contentment leads to less worry and less selfish behavior. It allows us to be more generous, to create more room to hear and follow Jesus, and to appreciate the simple joys in life.

In other words, contentment is absolutely worth pursuing. To understand more about how we can attain contentment, we're going to look at two passages in the Bible. The first is from Philippians.

The Secret of Contentment

Unless you're brand-new to the Christian faith, I would imagine you have heard some version of the Bible verse "I can do all this through him who gives me strength" (Philippians 4:13) many times. It is often quoted as an inspirational motto. We might use it in a general sense as encouragement to "dream big" or "believe the impossible." Athletes love to use it before a big game, as do people recently diagnosed with a terrible condition. I'm sure some Christians have even used it as justification for pouring their energies into getting rich and living large in a worldly sense.

But the phrase has a completely different meaning in its original context. What is this verse actually talking about? Experiencing contentment with our possessions.

That's right. The struggle that prompted Paul to first pen the statement "I can do all things through him who gives me strength" was about money and possessions. Here's the scenario:

While a prisoner in another city, the apostle Paul had received a financial gift from the believers of Philippi to help him out. So, he wrote a letter to thank them for this tangible display of their care.

It's interesting to me that at this point Paul wanted to make his attitude toward money very clear to the Philippians. As a prisoner who needed gifts from friends just to get by, he might have been feeling worried. Even desperate. Possibly eager for more so he could feel safer. But no. Paul felt . . . content.

"I am not saying this because I am in need," Paul explained, "for I have learned to be content whatever the circumstances. I know what it is to be in need, and I know what it is to have plenty. I have learned the secret of being content in any and every situation, whether well fed or hungry, whether living in plenty or in want" (verses 11–12).

Let's look closer, because there's a lot in this passage for us.

First, note that Paul said he had "learned" contentment. This implies that contentment doesn't come naturally to us. We're not born into it. In fact, our natural tendency is to be discontent, and the world feeds into that by constantly marketing products to us. So, contentment doesn't happen randomly or when we're not looking. We need to work on it and literally *learn* contentment. We have to seek it out, take intentional steps toward it—just like any other skill or value worth pursuing.

Second, Paul said that he had learned the "secret" of being content. Because it's a secret, it is not obvious to us. It's not common sense or knowledge or commonly promoted in our society. It remains elusive today just like in years past, if not even more so.

We see this in the world all around us. People desire contentment and talk about how great it is, yet somehow our houses get bigger, our closets get fuller, and our levels of personal debt continue to rise. The source of contentment is a secret that can be found only in the promise and presence of Christ—no worldly pursuit will ever uncover the truth.

Third, Paul says in this passage that he has learned to be content "in any and every situation, whether well fed or hungry, whether living in plenty or in want." One thing this implies is that no matter whether you're poor or wealthy, you can still be discontent or struggle to find contentment. Some of the wealthiest people in the world are the least content, and so are some of the poorest people in the world.

We of course know this to be true. We have money. Oh, we don't have as much as some other people in our neighborhoods, but what we do have is enough. We have opportunity; we have choices, yet . . . we're still buying stuff. We're still looking for more and better things. We're still chasing the next purchase that we think will finally make us happy. How can we ever get to the point of saying "I am satisfied with what I have" if we're acting like that?

Our state of contentment or the opposite is not based on our circumstances, but it is *exposed* in our circumstances. For those who are poor, discontentment means envy, and for those who have wealth, it means excess. Yet contentment can stretch to encompass people at every level of financial means too.

Now let's go back to the secret of contentment. What exactly *is* that secret?

It's not a technique to master.

It's not some kind of mind trick.

We find it in that popular verse "I can do all this *through him who gives me strength*" (verse 13, emphasis added). Through all that life has thrown at us so far, the good and the bad, have we learned that Christ is enough? We can be content in all circumstances of life because Christ gives us the ability and the formula to discover it. *He* is the secret. And He will never leave us nor forsake us.

How Contentment Leads to Ambition

Right here, I feel a need to head off a possible objection. There are some people who don't even want contentment, regardless of what its secret might be, because they're worried that it might lead to complacency.

But I have found the opposite to be true.

Contentment isn't about giving up or not wanting more. It's

actually a powerful force that can lay the groundwork and provide the inspiration to reach higher heights than we ever dreamed.

That is why God can tell us to both keep striving *and* practice contentment. When we read the Bible, we find phrases such as *press on toward the goal, run . . . the race, let us not become weary,* and *work at it with all your heart.*[3] We also see instructions or principles like *be content with what you have, godliness with contentment is great gain,* and *do not worry about your life, what you will eat or drink.*[4]

These thoughts—ambition and contentment—are not mutually exclusive. They can co-exist. And I'll even take this a step further: Not only can they both be present, but also godly contentment can *feed* our ambitions in life. Contentment with our individual lots in the world fuels our ambition for Him!

Contentment is mentioned three times in the New Testament (Philippians 4:11–12; 1 Timothy 6:6–10; and Hebrews 13:5). And all of them are in direct reference to money or possessions! The logic is this: Once you become content with the things of the world that you possess, you are freed to pursue the kingdom of God.

Contentment isn't about settling. It's about recognizing that you have enough, that it came from God, and that there are greater things to pursue than more of this world.

Correctly understood, it's acknowledging that while you have enough, you also have so much potential in the kingdom that's waiting to be unlocked.

It would be wise for all of us to redefine what it means to be content. Contentment isn't about giving up on our dreams or settling for less. It's about finding the freedom to become all that God desires us to be. It's about recognizing our full potential in Him, dreaming even bigger dreams for our lives, and channeling our resources into the most meaningful ambitions that will last for eternity.

He Is Enough

I promised you two key Bible passages that throw light on contentment in relation to our possessions. Let's get to the second one.

Hebrews 13:5 contains a fascinating combination of truths that provide us access and insight into the truest form of contentment in life. It is an experience of contentment that possessions can never provide.

The verse begins like this: "Keep your lives free from the love of money and be content with what you have." Or as I keep putting it in this book, have an *uncluttered faith* free from the pursuit of excess.

Remember, God always gives us His commands not because He's persnickety and insistent about rule keeping but because *they are good for us.* Just like a good father helps his child prepare to make the most of their life, so too does our heavenly Father. We can see that in His words here. Think about it: There is simply no joy to be found in constantly desiring things we do not have; joy is found in appreciating the blessings we already have around us.

So far, in telling us not to love money and to be content with what we have, this verse is not a big surprise. What is curious to me is the second half of the verse. This is where the writer tells us *why* we should replace greed and acquisitiveness with contentment. The explanation begins like this: "*Because God has said . . .*" (emphasis added).

Before I give you the rest of the wording, let me ask you: If you were writing this book of the Bible, how would you finish that verse? If you were counseling someone to be content and not love money, what promise of God might you offer to make your case? Would you remind them that God has said, "The love of money is a root of all kinds of evil" (1 Timothy 6:10)? Or maybe that He said not to worry about what you will eat or drink (Matthew 6:25)? Or that He loves us with an everlasting love (Jeremiah 31:3)?

As true as those things are, the author of Hebrews offers none of them. Instead, he refers to Deuteronomy 31:6, where God promises to "never leave you nor forsake you."

So, let's put it together. Why are we supposed to be content with what we have? Because *God has said He will never leave us nor forsake us.*

I think most of us believe God will always be with us—and we cherish that assurance. But what makes this particular promise the basis for a proper Christian approach to money and possessions?

I believe it is this: If the Giver of all hope and joy is *already* living inside and alongside us, what more could money and possessions add to our lives? They certainly can't bring us more joy or more hope. They can't bring us more purpose or fulfillment or security. Money and possessions can't add any of those things to our lives.

The God of all creation has already provided everything we need, and He will never leave us or forsake us! Daily and sufficiently, He offers all we need for life and godliness. The offerings of this world are at best a cheap substitute for what we have in our Lord. In Him, all the joy and satisfaction we could ask for are available to us day and night . . . forever.

If you are having a hard time receiving this, I want to direct your attention to the repeated word "never" in the Hebrews passage. For emphasis, God uses it twice in saying, "Never will I leave you; never will I forsake you."

Now, we tend to throw the word *never* around rather casually in our speech. "I would never eat that." "You would never catch me doing that." Yet there's a good possibility that we *would* eat or do those things under the right circumstances.

But when God says "never," He *means* "never."

He really will *never* leave us or forsake us.

You may be thinking, *But you don't know what mistakes I've made. You don't know what sin is in my life. You don't know how far I have run from God looking for happiness.*

That is true. But I know the promise of God in this verse. And if you are in Christ, you are a part of His family and God's promise applies to you. He will never leave you, and He will never forsake you. You have all you need in Him. You can be content—truly content.

Learning from Immigrants

I have had the privilege of traveling to poor areas of the world, and I have often been reminded of how people can be content and happy with far fewer things than we consider necessary. Samantha and Jesse Medina, of Houston, Texas, got the same insight without leaving their hometown.

A few years back, they were involved in a ministry outreach to an ethnic enclave of Houston known as the Mahatma Gandhi District. They served eight hundred apartments, occupied mostly by Hindu and Muslim families from India.

"We would enter their homes, which seemed so empty," remembers Samantha. "They would maybe have one couch, food in cabinets, and nothing else but their family inside. Most of them did not even own a bed and slept on the floor in one-room apartments with a family of maybe five, made up of three generations. These people came straight from India, and to them this apartment in Houston was *luxury*, even though they owned limited possessions. They seemed very happy but struggled spiritually. We were able to share Jesus's love and grace with them, and some came to know Christ."

Going into the homes, the Medinas would find the Indian families sitting there together on their one couch or sitting on the floor and peacefully enjoying life together. When these families came into the Medina home, they would comment on the abundance of stuff, just as the Medinas had noticed their absence of stuff. It all got the Medinas thinking.

"Our home was stuffed full of items," says Samantha, "and it felt as if we could never do family time since we were so busy picking up items, cleaning, and just trying to move stuff off tables and counters. Our small apartment was bursting at the seams with possessions I brought from my parents' home and items they bought for our newborn son."

She and her husband began researching and implementing minimalism. It changed their lives in ways they never could have expected.

"As more physical possessions leave our home, I become spiritually filled up in Christ. Now I am able to read my Bible without distractions. I can have devotion time with my children and husband, since the only things in our living room are two couches, a wood bench, a small buffet table, and their Bibles and a few folded blankets. Each day it's freeing to know we can easily and quickly find our Bibles and start reading them."

Enough is more than too much. (Reread that sentence if you need to.) By getting their possessions down to the necessary, the Medinas are enjoying a contentment and satisfaction they glimpsed before but had never fully experienced for themselves. It's good for them and for those who know them.

Samantha says, "It is freeing to focus on what matters most: the Lord, my family, and others in our community."

Wanting Less

In her book *You Can Never Get Enough of What You Don't Need*, Mary Ellen Edmunds says, "Wanting less is probably a better blessing than having more."[5] Mary Ellen's words caused me to see the pursuit of possessions in a new way. As I began to notice, it is one thing to own less; it is something completely different to *want* less.

There are many who want to declutter and organize, but if they don't overcome the desire to acquire more, their houses will quickly fill up with stuff again. It is only when we conquer our yearnings for more consumer goods and genuinely desire to own less that we can experience the greatest benefits of minimalism.

"Wanting less" is another way of referring to contentment. It's being satisfied that enough is enough. Your ambition isn't squelched by contentment—it's redirected and fueled for greater things! But as far as your material status goes, you're good with what you have.

That feeling you get when you push back from the Thanksgiving dinner table, full and satisfied and wanting no more? You can have it all the time if you minimize.

15

More than Happy

If you had asked me before I became a minimalist, "Joshua, what brings you joy?" I would have said emphatically, "God does. Knowing Him and serving Him is where I find my joy. The Lord is the only source of true joy in the universe."

But did my life really reflect that?

The truth is, the way I spent my money, along with the ever-increasing number of possessions in our house, said otherwise. Becoming minimalist revealed this inconsistency to me. Without fully recognizing it before then, I had been seeking joy in the Lord *and* in things. That never works.

Jesus said it this way: "You cannot serve God and mammon" (Matthew 6:24, NKJV). Nor can you rely on both to bring you joy. You always wind up trading off one for the other somehow.

Importantly, although it is sometimes translated "money," *mammon* actually has a wider meaning. It refers to riches in general, including our property and earthly goods.[1] All these are things of this world that can divert our attention from God to earthly desires.

Since adopting an uncluttered faith, I've changed. I'm no longer looking to buy and own things to give me happiness. I can now truthfully say more of my life is aligned with the reality that God gives me joy above all things. *Happiness* isn't even an adequate word for it; only *joy—lasting joy*—comes close to describing the actual experience.

Yet I know that many fellow Christians are stuck in a place similar to where I used to be. Even with good intentions, they are subtly confusing their sources of delight. They assume they can love, worship, and adore Jesus while at the same time busily construct luxurious lifestyles that they think will bring them happiness on this earth. They go to church on Sunday morning and hear all about the needs God wants to use them to meet, and then they drive home to park in their two-car garages, turn on their seventy-five-inch flatscreen TVs, watch football all afternoon, and order Uber Eats for dinner.

Do you have more things in your home than you need? I hate to say this, but it's probably a sign that your affections are tied up more with worldly desires than you would prefer to admit. Maybe you're, at best, inconsistent in seeking joy in the Lord, same as I was.

Minimalism shows us what's going on in our hearts. I'm not just talking about how removing physical possessions simultaneously removes distractions from God, although that is true. Even better, minimalism redirects us from unworthy to more worthy pursuits of joy. Best yet, it keeps us from falling back into a futile pursuit of happiness in things—if our minimalism is permanent, so can be our priority on God.

Physical possessions don't bring real joy; they are a hindrance to it. They provide only fleeting pleasure, even though the world tells us constantly to spend our resources in pursuit of joy. But in a culture predisposed to seek happiness in physical possessions, it can be hard to recognize it in ourselves. Embracing the teachings of Jesus on possessions and money allows us to finally find the real, lasting joy in God that our souls are longing for.

The Expanding Balloon

To be a kid in the 1980s almost inevitably meant you were obsessed with Nintendo gaming. With Christmas coming up in 1987, my brother and I—junior highers at the time—informed our parents that we "just had to have" the NES Advantage, Nintendo's new controller. It had a joystick like an arcade game, turbo controls for the A and B buttons, plus a SLOW button to turn game action into a kind of slow motion so you could beat the hardest levels. It sounded amazing!

After presents started showing up under the Christmas tree that year, Jerrod and I noticed a wrapped package that was just the right size, shape, and weight—clearly it was an Advantage.

One evening, when our parents were out of the home for a seasonal event, one of us suggested to the other that we open the Advantage and play with it. It was my brother's idea. (Mom or Dad, if you're reading this, that is absolutely how the story went down!)

We got out the game controller, hooked it up to our Nintendo system, and started playing. We were so excited. And it turned out that the NES Advantage was . . . all right. It wasn't as cool as we'd been led to believe. In particular, the slow-motion feature, which I'd been especially looking forward to, didn't even work on most of my favorite games.

By the time my brother and I rewrapped the toy to put it back under the Christmas tree, we were already disappointed in it. This was going to make our simulated surprise and happiness when we opened it on Christmas morning that much more difficult to pull off.

Probably every one of us can remember at least one toy from childhood that lost its appeal with unexpected speed. As adults, we have the same kind of experience, just with different kinds of products. After driving a junker and saving up money, a buyer revels in their new car . . . for a while . . . until it gets its first door ding or they spill their first cup of coffee on its upholstery. A couple may replace the secondhand furniture in their family room with a complete new set they saw in a showroom, and it looks so good . . . for a while . . . until they don't notice it anymore. We love our new phones . . . for a while . . . until the next models come out. I believe those are all the examples I need to mention, because I expect you already recognize the phenomenon I'm talking about. I bet you can think of more than one recent purchase that took you on a fast ride from *Wow!* to *Meh.*

This phenomenon is so common to human nature that it has a name: *hedonic adaptation.* One scientific definition goes like this: "Hedonic adaptation refers to the notion that after positive (or negative) events (i.e., something good or bad happening to someone), and a subsequent increase in positive (or negative feelings), people return to a relatively stable, baseline level of affect."[2]

In other words, stuff disappoints. The tang of happiness that a new purchase releases for us quickly dissipates, leaving us looking for the next acquisitions that we hope will deliver bursts of good feelings. At some point, we either recognize it and step off the treadmill or live lifestyles of forever collecting more and more.

And this leads to another phenomenon we're all familiar with: *lifestyle inflation* (or *lifestyle creep*). "Lifestyle inflation," says Investopedia, "occurs when your spending rises to keep pace with a situational change, such as . . . receiving a pay increase. Instead of having extra money to save, you find yourself spending it instead. Though you've earned more money, it doesn't feel like more money because you've spent it."[3]

Here's how that looked for my family. Our starter home in Wisconsin had two bedrooms and one bathroom in 1,200 square feet. Our second home added both a bedroom and a bathroom and was 1,800 square feet. Our third home, in Vermont, had four bedrooms and two and a half baths in 2,300 square feet.[4] This just seemed like the natural progression we were supposed to take.

And most of us follow a similar trajectory—not just with our homes but with lots of other kinds of possessions—as our income increases.

We add outfits, with more colors and styles, to our wardrobes.

We upgrade to the latest technological devices.

We gradually fill our jewelry boxes with more and pricier bling.

Instead of eating at home most of the time, we go to restaurants frequently, at first fast-food joints and gradually fancier restaurants.

We buy boats or ATVs or RVs just because they seem fun.

But here's the thing: With all these purchases, we aren't getting closer to lasting happiness. We never get to a place where we say, "Ah, now I'm perfectly satisfied and content with my collection of stuff." We experience some enjoyment along the way, but a letdown follows close on the heels of each hit of pleasure.

I know this is true of you—because it's true of everybody! Worldly possessions never fully satisfy our hearts and souls. They always leave us wanting more.

With all this lifestyle inflation, you could say our material possessions are like expanding balloons. Some of us just keep letting our balloons get bigger and bigger, regardless of how overstuffed they are. Others of us reach a point, for one reason or another, where we can't stand the tension anymore. We burst our balloons by saying no to the constant hedonic adaptation and lifestyle inflation; we minimize our possessions, seeking a happiness that has nothing to do with material ownership.

That is my hope with this book. To pop the ever-expanding balloon in your life so you can replace it with real, lasting joy.

Of course, wherever you choose to look for joy other than physical possessions is up to you. I know many minimalists, typically outside the church, choose to seek happiness in various worldly pursuits. There may be good in some of those. But they fall short of lasting joy. That can be found only in Christ.

There is no hedonic adaptation in our relationship with the Lord. In fact, the opposite is true. His nature is infinite, so our enjoyment of Him never ceases but grows.

One of the most marvelous truths I ever heard about God came from eighteenth-century theologian Jonathan Edwards when he explained how, because God is an infinite being, He is the source of infinite joy. In other words, the joy we find in God is ever expanding, with no end. Edwards said, "The more they love God, the more delight and happiness . . . will they have in him."[5]

In heaven, we will grow in joy more and more each day for all eternity. Imagine that: increasing joy every day for all of eternity! But we don't have to wait for heaven to begin this enjoyment. We can begin *today* growing in "delight and happiness."

First Peter says the heavenly Father has given us a new birth into "an inheritance that can never perish, spoil or fade" (1:4). Because of this, we are "filled with an inexpressible and glorious joy" (verse 8). There are no words for the joy we can know in God's presence, because there is no end to His glory.

Once we have our vision cleared of the fog of consumerism

and can see the vast difference between the fleeting enjoyment of things and lasting joy in God, we'll be ready to drop the one to seize the other.

The Bargain of a Lifetime

By this point in *Uncluttered Faith,* we've already looked at many Bible passages and have seen how a minimalist perspective can open up previously unnoticed insights into those passages. Now let's look at another few verses from the Gospels. Do these twin mini-parables take on new context and meaning for you when you read them through the lens of simplicity?

- **The parable of the hidden treasure:** "The kingdom of heaven is like treasure hidden in a field. When a man found it, he hid it again, and then in his joy *went* and *sold all* he had and bought that field" (Matthew 13:44, emphasis added).
- **The parable of the pearl:** "Again, the kingdom of heaven is like a merchant looking for fine pearls. When he found one of great value, *he went away* and *sold everything* he had and bought it" (verses 45–46, emphasis added).

It is not hard to see that these parables represent minimalism in practice. Each describes the exact same decision and action—both men sold "all" or "everything" they had. Like us getting rid of whatever possessions get in the way of becoming like Jesus and fulfilling our godly callings, these story characters were willing to sell off the unnecessary.

And *why* did they do this? Because each had found something better! For one man it was buried treasure, and for the other it was an exceptional pearl. Both prizes represent the same thing: the kingdom of heaven. This goal was more valuable than *all* the things the two men had accumulated throughout the lifestyle inflation of their years.

Notice, too, that neither man had the option of holding on to his things *and* acquiring the prize. Each man had to give up the one to get the other. Yet both realized the trade-off was more than worth it.

In the first parable, we specifically learn that the man went "in his joy" to sell his things and buy the field containing the treasure. I imagine a man excitedly offering his donkey for sale to a neighbor. Or smiling as he carts his grain stores into town on market day. Or announcing the news that he's putting his house up for sale.

The neighbors may have wondered what was going on with this guy suddenly selling off everything the world had told him to accumulate and seeming happy to be doing it. But no amount of arguing would change his mind. Because inside he was bubbling with anticipation of the life-altering transaction he was about to make. Going about his business during the day or lying in bed at night, he couldn't get the image of that buried wealth off his mind.

For him, getting rid of his possessions was no exercise in self-denial for the sake of it. He was doing it because he was going to get something greater. He was about to become the possessor of the greatest treasure any of us could discover!

No wonder Jesus is so adamant throughout the New Testament in commanding us to sell our possessions. The treasure—Himself—awaits on the other side.

Let me be unmistakably clear here that minimalism is not itself the treasure or the pearl. The prize is the kingdom of heaven. Minimalism is a crucial intermediate step we take toward fully taking hold of the riches that God offers to all who belong to Him through trusting in the King, Jesus.

I fear too many of us are trying to have both. We have found the pearl in Jesus Christ. We can see its value is far greater than anything this world could ever offer, yet we are unwilling to sell off everything to attain it. Satan has convinced us we can have both. But we are being deceived. Although we desire the great treasure of Christ in our lives, we are unwilling to take the steps required to attain it.

The Kingdom of God Versus the Kingdom of Things

Oswald Chambers tells us this:

> The cares of this world, said Jesus, will choke God's word. Before we know where we are, we are caught up in the shows of things. All that God has done for us is the mere threshold; He wants to get us to the place where we will be His witnesses and proclaim Who Jesus is.
>
> Be rightly related to God, find your joy there, and out of you will flow rivers of living water.[6]

If you need any convincing that he's right, let's dive deeper in to the trade-off we are invited to make.

- Owning an expensive car might turn heads and make people admire you for a moment. But in Christ you are called a royal priest, a part of the chosen people, and a child of the King.
- Luxury vacations offer a temporary escape from stress and

look good on social media. But Jesus offers something infinitely greater: true rest and a peace that passes understanding.

- A fashionable wardrobe might help you look put together on the world's runway. But being clothed in the armor of God prepares you for spiritual victory.
- A well-funded retirement account might offer some semblance of security and peace of mind. But true peace comes from knowing God has promised to meet all your needs—just like He watches over the sparrow and the lily.
- Expensive jewelry might sparkle for a night. But Jesus offers you treasure where neither moth nor rust destroys and where thieves don't break in and steal.
- A big house might impress your guests. But an even greater home is available whose architect and builder is God.
- An ever-packed schedule of worldly pursuits might sound like the path to fulfillment. But Jesus offers you *a yoke that is easy and light.*

The Best Way

Ruth Shetler was listening to the audiobook *The Ruthless Elimination of Hurry* by John Mark Comer, where he discusses how following Jesus means living the way He did. One of those ways of living involves simplicity and minimalism.

"I walked into our house after listening to the book," Ruth recalls, "and truly looked at the possessions filling our house, as well as the calendar overflowing with to-dos and activities. It was no wonder that anxiety greeted me every time I opened our door. I realized then how much of the Kool-Aid I had drunk, how much consumerism did plague my life. This was not what Jesus had taught or modeled. This had to change."

Ruth researched minimalism, including taking my Uncluttered course, and began letting go of things she had held on to for years. In eight months she went through her family's whole house and gave away thousands of items.

Then she and her husband decided to move with their little ones from their 1,700-square-foot house to a 1,056-square-foot home.

"Now that we are in a smaller house, I feel joy and peace, seeing the fruit of all the hard decisions. Life without all the extra possessions is truly freeing. No more mental noise and anxiety screaming from the clutter. No more pull to accumulate and keep pace with a culture that is never satisfied. There is calm where there once was always a storm.

"Minimalism has acted like windshield wipers. It has removed the distractions so that I can see more clearly what God is offering. And once you see what He is offering, it is impossible to go back to staring at dirty water spots.

"God's way is truly the best way."

Eyes on a Higher Prize

The goal of our God-motivated minimalism is progress, not perfection. As long as we live in a fallen world and battle against a sinful nature, we are going to make mistakes. That is where the grace of Christ covers us. Before I end up painting an inaccurate picture of my life, I want you to know that this is something I still struggle with.

After I published my first book, *The More of Less,* I went on a book tour to several cities to promote the new release. My family went with me—we turned it into a kind of vacation. Before we left, I thought it would be a good idea to buy an expensive camera so one of us could capture moments from the tour (Joshua on stage, crowd sizes, book signings) as well as a few of the activities we'd do as a family on the trip.

You might guess how this story ends.

When we got back from the tour and looked at the pictures, I suddenly realized why people take courses and even get degrees in photography. Honestly, the photos we'd taken with the new camera were no better than the ones we had taken with our phones. There had really been no point in getting the camera. It was as big a letdown as that NES Advantage so many years ago.

So, to be clear: I gave in to the lures of lifestyle creep by buying this camera and then experienced rapid hedonic adaptation with it. *And all on a trip to promote minimalism!*

The temptations to look for happiness where it doesn't lie never stop coming at us. We get better at spotting these temptations and resisting them, but we can't give up our vigilance. The most important part in this vigilance isn't sticking to a minimalism plan; it's remembering the joy that is ours when we set our hearts fully on Christ and not on the things of the world.

If you were to ask Jesus, "Lord, why do You want me to follow Your commands, including those to sell my possessions?" I believe He would say, "So that my joy may be in you and that your joy may be complete" (John 15:11).

16

Shine a Brighter Light

Jesus was a minimalist, and His kingdom is a spiritual one, where creating our own little empires makes no sense and is just a squandering of resources. Jesus's frequent theme of selling our possessions is one of the great overlooked messages in the New Testament, directly addressing one of the great overlooked sins in American life today: complacency in the overaccumulation of money and things. And if we do what Jesus says about de-owning and living more simply for His kingdom, we'll be using an often-overlooked key to open up a much fuller experience of the abundant life God graciously offers us in His Son.

What, specifically, are the benefits of an uncluttered faith? I've described a round dozen of them (and there are more I could have gone into!):

- learning about yourself (chapter 4)
- walking closer with Jesus (chapter 5)
- overcoming greed (chapter 6)

- moving past worry (chapter 7)
- living more intentionally (chapter 8)
- prioritizing spiritual growth (chapter 9)
- building better relationships (chapter 10)
- redefining success (chapter 11)
- seeing work differently (chapter 12)
- being more generous (chapter 13)
- discovering contentment (chapter 14)
- experiencing lasting joy (chapter 15)

In light of these benefits, if you still haven't minimized, get started today. Or if you're in the process, keep going. The blessings on the other side of obedience to Jesus's call to voluntary simplicity are amazing! I want you to have them. More to the issue, God wants that for you!

And now I want to make one last point and invite you to consider another spiritual benefit: Your minimalism will provide you with opportunities to influence others for Christ. Both nonbelievers and believers will be intrigued by the things they see in you if you'll make the new minimalist version of you transparent for them. As we said in a previous chapter, make the most of every opportunity.

A. W. Tozer wrote, "If we cooperate with Him in loving obedience, God will manifest Himself to us, and that manifestation will be the difference between a nominal Christian life and a life radiant with the light of His face."[1] What if he is literally right about that? That our obedience to Christ in this area will reflect the light of God to others?

God wants an abundant life for others too.

Are You a Missionary?

In 2018, I spoke at a professional organizers' conference in São Paulo, Brazil. As part of the event, which was held at a large convention center, I was assigned a personal security guard, Gabriel. He and I spent the day together, moving from one responsibility to another.

After my keynote presentation that evening, Gabriel and I found ourselves alone in the greenroom for a short time. He turned to me and asked a question—the first thing he said to me all day: "Joshua, are you a missionary?"

It was a surprising question—almost shocking. I certainly wasn't expecting it. To be honest, I wasn't sure of his intent in asking it or whether the word *missionary* meant the same thing to him as it did to me. So, I asked for clarification.

"What do you mean by 'missionary'?"

He replied, "I've been watching you interact with people all day. And when I heard you speak onstage today about minimalism, I sensed that your message was about something more. The Lord told me while you were speaking that you have been sent here by Him. You love to talk about minimalism, but your greatest passion is leading people to Christ, isn't it? I am a Christian, too, and I want to thank you."

That was the only time a compliment following a presentation ever brought me to tears.

I hadn't talked about Jesus at all onstage. Yet I was reminded that evening that minimalism can be about a lot more than decluttering.

As believers, we each have a light shining within us—the light of Christ. I believe that if we let them, our new uncluttered lifestyles will enable us to stand out even more in the world, making Christ's light shine a little brighter.

The Privilege of Being Different

As followers of Jesus, we are called to live differently from the world. As you know, this is not a burden—it's a privilege.

In the Sermon on the Mount, Jesus paints a picture of the life available to us.

> You are the light of the world. A town built on a hill cannot be hidden. Neither do people light a lamp and put it under a bowl. Instead they put it on its stand, and it gives light to everyone in the house. In the same way, let your light shine before others, that they may see your good deeds and glorify your Father in heaven. (Matthew 5:14–16)

We are the light of the world. A town or city on a hill, visible for all to see. A lamp on a stand, lighting up a house. What an amazing opportunity! What a joy!

The world around us is broken, filled with sin and darkness. And the consequences of this fallen world are clear: debt, anxiety, burnout, addiction. But when we live set apart—when we follow God's commands and let our light shine—we are given the incredible privilege of reflecting God's goodness and truth.

Think about what it means to be "the light of the world." Jesus is not calling us to hide or blend into the darkness. Just the opposite. He's calling us to stand out, to live in a way that is so attractive, so distinct, so different from the world's standards that others can't help but notice and be drawn to it.

Now, there are many ways in which we can stand out in the world as a city on a hill.

For one thing, we may stand out by living according to God's design for our lives—using our power not to manipulate others but to serve them. We stand out in the way we talk. We stand out by pursuing sexual purity. Or going about our work with integrity and in truth. Behaviors like these make us different from the world around us, noticeable and set apart.

Then there's how we treat people. The Jesus way of life boils down to love, so it is no surprise that Jesus said, "By this everyone will know that you are my disciples, if you love one another" (John 13:35). We seek to serve rather than be served. We pursue unity and peace in a society growing increasingly divided.

But in a world consumed by the pursuit of money and possessions, there is another way we can stand out: through minimalism—owning less, being content with what we have, and choosing bigger dreams for our lives. The more effort society puts into accumulating more and more things, the greater our opportunity to stand out as a city on a hill when we reject all of it.

While most people around us are striving for more money and are obsessed with accumulating things, we reject the world's trinkets and pursue treasures of eternal and infinite worth.

We become light through minimalism because it changes

- how we spend our money,
- how we spend our time,
- how we define success,
- what we are passionate about,
- how we view work, and
- how we define the goal of our lives.

We follow a Savior who talked about losing your life to find it. Who urged us to take up our crosses daily. Who, in the Beatitudes, defined happiness in an upside-down manner, boldly proclaiming, "Blessed are the poor, the meek, the merciful, and the peacemakers" (see Matthew 5). A Savior who had every opportunity to take as much of the world as He desired but laid it all down for the sake of His Father in heaven.

Minimalism is consistent with Jesus's surprising, countercultural perspective. It draws people to Him. Materialism does not. A materialistic Christian directs attention back to the world and casts a dim light illuminating the wrong things.

Put your light on a stand so it can shine for others. This doesn't mean pridefully drawing attention to yourself or bragging to others about your minimalist lifestyle. Sometimes it's just about following God's countercultural plan faithfully and letting others observe what you're about—then you'll stand out naturally.

Am I overstating the potential of this lifestyle? I don't think so.

Not every person you pass on the street will recognize your minimalism. But you know who will? Your kids and spouse will, and so will your friends and extended family. Your boss and coworkers will eventually notice. Even your neighbors will spot it. (The number of neighbors who have commented to me about the lack of boxes in my garage is staggering.) Minimalism is just different. And the closer you are to somebody, the sooner they will recognize something different about your attitude and approach to the world and consumeristic pursuits.

There are people in your life who you can love and serve better than anyone else can. It is essential that we never forget, as my friend Andy Pauwels says, "God has placed each of us near someone who is far from God." Our countercultural lifestyle provides an opening to shine a light for them.

The more materialistic the world becomes, the greater our opportunity to stand out in it.

When we're making any kind of positive change in our lives, such as starting an exercise routine or self-limiting our phone use, we tend to talk about it. Why shouldn't it be the same way with minimizing, especially if we're doing it with the desire to please God?

Sometimes Words Speak Louder than Actions

The apostle Peter said, "Live such good lives among the pagans that, though they accuse you of doing wrong, they may see your good deeds and glorify God on the day he visits us" (1 Peter 2:12). People are naturally curious about others (if not downright nosy). That's one reason to be intentional about our faithfulness to God's ways: because people are watching. Among other "good deeds," your minimalism will be a silent witness to people that you are striving for heavenly rather than earthly values.

Peter tells us in 1 Peter 3:15 that we should also have a verbal witness ready to go: "Always be prepared to give an answer to everyone who asks you to give the reason for the hope that you have." Not every conversation you have about minimalism will result in your talking about God, but some of them might. And when they do, you can be ready.

Knowing your simple living is going to provoke curiosity in others, be prepared to share the reasons why your faith in God inspires you to live with less stuff. You might include statements like these:

- "To be honest, my faith plays a huge role in how I view money and possessions. This is one of the ways it plays out."
- "As you know, I'm a Christian. And the more I look at the

life of Jesus, the more compelled I am to live for Him. Minimalism is an extension of that."
- "My time on this earth is too precious to waste on things that don't have eternal meaning."
- "When I realized that I wasn't finding joy in stuff, it forced me to think about where I *could* find joy. My joy is in God."
- "I want to devote more of my resources to supporting the kingdom of God, by volunteering my time and donating money. Minimalism makes that possible."
- "I'm just trying to be faithful to God with my money and time."

Minimizing gives you a natural, credible opportunity to talk about God and your belief in Him. Wouldn't it be great to introduce someone to both simplicity and the Savior?

Passing It On

I've been speaking in this chapter mainly about being a light to those who don't yet know God personally through His Son. But along with that, minimalism will provide us opportunity to be a source of encouragement, inspiration, and challenge to our fellow believers about the connection between living simply and experiencing more of the blessings of Christ. We can spread the message and promise of minimalism to others.

Trish Croyle had the good fortune to grow up living next door to her grandparents in northern New Jersey. Her grandmother was her best friend. Trish would spend hours at Nana's house, enjoying the simple life.

Trish recalls, "She woke up every morning, collected eggs

from her chickens, picked vegetables from her garden, and picked berries from her berry patches. We would spend hours playing cards, 500 rum or solitaire, or watching the birds eating from her feeders.

"As I got older, I would continue to visit her. In the morning I'd go for a run and come back to Nana sitting on her sunporch, praying. We would go into the kitchen, and always waiting for me was a big bowl of freshly picked berries."

Inspired by her grandmother, Trish today lives a simple, faith-filled life. She has chickens, a garden, and berry patches. She and her husband play cards and board games with their four children. Every time she watches the birds at the feeders, she remembers her now-departed nana.

"My grandmother's quiet, simple faith has been my foundation in my faith," says Trish. "I know I was so fortunate to have such an amazing role model in Nana."

When you model or talk about your minimalism with fellow believers, who knows? You might be inspiring them to join you in an uncluttered faith.

I believe that, beginning now, a return to biblical minimalism might spread and grow from generation to generation within the family of faith, as it was passed to Trish from her nana. It can spread from friend to friend. From church to church. Naturally, organically, and by word of mouth, minimalism—by virtue of its power to take us out of worldly distraction and restore us to the blessed Jesus way—can reform the nature of everyday Christian living here and around the world.

Will you help?

Jesus's words are the words of life. You can show others in your own circle of relationships that when we follow Jesus's teaching about giving up our excess possessions and being more generous, it is not a sacrifice of our own happiness. It is instead an indispensable way to receive more of the abundant life than we've ever known. We can only imagine its full potential.

Uncluttered Church

After living more than fifteen years as a minimalist and seeing how it has helped people of all backgrounds, and now after having written a book to my fellow Jesus lovers urging us all to return to our original calling to live without unnecessary entanglements with the world and its distractions, I'm dreaming about what could be. I've taken my message to many churches and seen faces light up with understanding. I believe I've discerned some movement within Christian ranks toward minimalism, especially among the younger generations but also among the older.

What if, in large numbers, we took up minimalism? How would it change the body of Christ? And how would the body of Christ then change the world?

Dream with me about what this would mean for our families, our communities, our nations, and the ever-eternal kingdom of God.

Imagine a church—the worldwide church—uncluttered, unburdened with excess possessions, and more alive with purpose. I've spent years dreaming about this, and the more I ponder it, the more I believe it's not just a possibility; it's an opportunity hidden in plain sight within the teachings of Jesus. If you have been inspired by this book, buy another copy for someone who would benefit from its message.

Picture this: a church that becomes more fruitful, both in reaching people for Christ and in caring for the least of these. With fewer possessions tying us down, we'd have more time, more energy, and more resources to share the gospel and "to look after orphans and widows in their distress and to keep [ourselves] from being polluted by the world" (James 1:27).

We'd become a people more united in love—not because all our differences would vanish but because, as we relied on one another and shared what we have, our hearts would grow together in ways that transcend theological debates or political differences. We would be known by everyone because we'd love one another. Competition would fade too—between individuals chasing status and between churches as well. Jesus, as the head of the body, could again become our focus. We'd cheer each other on, celebrating every soul reached and every life restored.

And the money! Oh, the resources that would flow if we stopped using them to pursue and accumulate the physical world around us. Ministries would thrive; church plants would spring up in our towns, in our regions, and around the globe. We'd be freed up financially and mentally to actually solve problems around the world, not just send pennies on the dollar.

The great city on a hill, the hope of the nations, would glow brighter and brighter as our attention turned from our individual kingdoms to Jesus's everlasting kingdom. The light would grow unmistakably bright as the Lord added to our number daily those who were being saved (see Acts 2:47).

I picture a church that calls out in the wilderness, boldly speaking truth to a materialistic world—not with judgment and negativity but with the power of lives that are different because we have tasted what is good. As a body, we would better know the only true God, and Jesus Christ whom He has sent (see John 17:3). No doubt, our love would "abound more and more in knowledge and depth of insight . . . to the glory and praise of God" (Philippians 1:9, 11).

This is a dream for the church. But it is not unrealistic. It is a return to the simplicity lived out by Jesus and laid out in God's Word. His words are "useful for teaching, rebuking, correcting and training in righteousness, so that [we] may be thoroughly equipped for every good work" (2 Timothy 3:16–17).

You've read these pages, felt the tug of this uncluttered faith. Now let's take it further. Let's own less together. Not just today but for the rest of our lives. And not just for our own blessing but for the world's. This church could change everything. Will you join me?

b o n u s

The Becker Method: A Seven-Step Guide to Becoming Minimalist

Throughout *Uncluttered Faith,* I've explained the spiritual benefits available to us when we begin living out Jesus's specific teachings related to material possessions. This is a weighty topic—one with genuine life change attached to it. Because here is the real abundant life, one that is not obsessed with things but rich toward God. I've seen the change in my own life and in countless others. You, too, can experience those blessings.

But how? You may be wondering, *How do I start? Where do I begin?*

This guide is your answer. Literally from the first step to the last step, I want to provide you with everything you need to know.

I have presented bits and pieces of this approach to minimizing elsewhere. I have written an entire book on the process: *The Minimalist Home.* And I have been training professional declutterers and organizers in my methods for many years. But in this appendix, for the first time ever, I am going to present this seven-step plan in the most complete yet succinct way possible.

Don't confuse its succinctness with its effectiveness. These principles are quick to learn but will take much longer to apply.

Over the past fifteen years, I've had the privilege of helping millions of people declutter their homes and lives through a simple, proven method. Whether you're feeling overwhelmed by clutter and struggling to know where to start or you've been pursuing minimalism for a decade and are looking for new ideas to implement, you'll find your answers here.

The journey to minimalism is deeply personal—minimalism will look different in your life than it does in anyone else's—but these steps will get you there.

Step 1: Find your motivation.

Before you pick up a single item to declutter, take a moment to ask yourself, *Why do I want to own less?* This question is the foundation of your journey and the best, most important place to start. Minimizing your possessions is hard work, and there will be times when you are tempted to quit. But when that happens, this step will provide you with the motivation to keep going.

The motivation of owning less just for its own sake runs out pretty quickly. Getting very clear on the deeper motivation behind our desire to own less will keep us focused longer. And the more specific, the better. In this book, I have described twelve specific spiritual benefits that enter our lives as we own less. Did one of them stick out to you more than the others? Or maybe your motivation is even more specific: You'd like to spend more time with your kids, volunteer more at church, or get out of debt to discover more financial freedom and well-being. Each of those can be powerful motivators.

Here's a simple exercise to help you uncover your motivation. Complete this sentence: "I desire to own less so I can . . ." Once you decide on something, write it down and place the note somewhere visible—on your fridge, your bathroom mirror, or your phone's lock screen. When the process feels challenging, this statement will serve as a reminder of why you started.

Whenever you feel tempted to give up, return to your why. It will keep you grounded and focused on the bigger picture. Likewise, the more visible it is and the more often you see it, the more motivated you will become to make quick progress.

Step 2: Stay focused on the positives.

Decluttering can be emotional. Letting go of possessions—even those we no longer use—can stir up feelings of guilt, nostalgia, or fear. There are a lot of reasons we accumulate more than we need, and learning what those reasons are in our individual lives can be painful at times.

That is why it is so important to focus on the positives at the beginning and throughout this process. Rather than dwelling on what you're losing, celebrate what you're gaining. Instead of being motivated by the negatives of consumerism, you'll find greater momentum by thinking about the positives of minimalism. That is why this book has focused exclusively on the spiritual benefits and blessings of owning less.

For example, as you declutter, remind yourself of the benefits you're creating:

- More physical space in your home
- Less time spent cleaning and organizing

- Increased financial opportunities
- Reduced stress and mental clutter
- Or anything else from the chapters in this book!

Even positives like these can be helpful to think about:

- An easier time picking out clothes in the morning
- More counter space to cook on
- Ability to park in the garage again

When you focus on the positives, decluttering becomes less about losing the life you had and more about creating a new life focused on the things that matter most. Minimalism is actually more about adding good things to our lives than about removing unnecessary stuff.

Once you begin the process of minimizing, you will feel and experience the benefits quickly and almost immediately. I even have an entire step (step 5) dedicated to that because I think it is so important. But focusing more on the positives than the negatives at the very beginning is an essential and intentional mindset we all need. That's why it gets its own step in this process.

Step 3: Begin decluttering with a quick sweep.

Now it's time to take action and begin removing things from your home. But before you dive in to a full-scale decluttering project, start with a quick sweep of your entire home. This step is all about building momentum and getting comfortable with letting go.

If minimalism is new to you, it is during this step that you will first need to confront your tendency to organize rather than minimize. Organizing happens when we simply move items from one room or bin to a different one. There is a time and a place for organizing. But Jesus never called us to organize our stuff better. He called us to follow His example in owning only what we need.

If you find yourself falling into the trap of merely shuffling things around rather than moving them out the door of your home and life, here are four helpful thoughts to reframe your thinking:

- Organizing our stuff is only a temporary solution. But minimizing our possessions is a permanent act of freeing up time, space, and life.
- Organizing our stuff doesn't allow our excess to bless anyone else. But minimizing our possessions allows them to be donated and used by people in need.
- Organizing our stuff never results in the required internal work to overcome consumerism in our lives. But minimizing our possessions forces us to ask questions of why we bought and kept what we did and why some items are so difficult for us to remove.
- Organizing our stuff never results in life change. Moving things around to different places in the home changes our lives and our homes none whatsoever. But minimizing our possessions blazes a pathway for lasting life change and spiritual benefits.

Here's how the quick sweep works: Grab a box or bag, and walk through your home, looking for items that are easy to part with. Fill as many bags and/or boxes as you can with things like these from every area in your home:

- Broken or unused items
- Things you've been meaning to donate or throw away

- Duplicates (like extra kitchen utensils or old phone chargers)
- Items you know you'll never miss
- Plain old trash (expired coupons, junk mail, etc.)

The goal isn't to declutter your entire home in one go; it's to make a quick, visible impact. You may open closets and drawers during this step, but this isn't about going through every item in your home. It's about quickly scanning for things you can remove without any difficult decisions.

By removing these low-hanging-fruit items, you'll create immediate progress and build confidence. It's also a great way to get used to seeing things leave your home. For many of us, this can feel uncomfortable at first. But as you experience the freedom of letting go, you'll begin to see decluttering as a positive, empowering process.

Step 4: Declutter room by room, easiest to hardest, starting with lived-in areas.

With the quick sweep under your belt, you're ready to tackle your home systematically, room by room. This step is where the real transformation happens, and it's all about strategy. Let's spend a little more time here to make sure you understand the method.

Why room by room works best

There are three key reasons why decluttering room by room is the most effective approach:

1. **It leans in to the progress principle.** The progress principle suggests that when we see meaningful progress from a task or behavior, we are more likely to keep engaging in it,

and our productivity increases.[1] As an example, if you start a diet and step on the scale to see you've lost three pounds after the first couple of days, you become motivated to continue the behavior. In other words, progress fuels progress. By decluttering one room at a time (especially in spaces you spend time in), you'll have quick, observable wins that keep you motivated and build momentum for the next space.

2. **It prevents overwhelm.** Overwhelm happens when we focus on too big a project in too little time. That's why seeing your entire home as one giant decluttering project can feel paralyzing. But when you break it down into smaller, manageable pieces—one room at a time—the task becomes less daunting and more achievable.

3. **It keeps your home usable.** Decluttering room by room keeps you from making your entire home a mess at one time (and for an extended period). Rather than trying to declutter every space in your home at once, by focusing on one room at a time, you'll keep the rest of your home functional.

The road map for success

For a majority of people, the most effective way to minimize possessions room by room is to start with the easiest, most lived-in areas and gradually move to the more challenging ones.

You'll notice two qualifiers to this approach: *easiest* and *most lived-in*. Beginning with the spaces where you spend the most time—like the living room, bedroom, and kitchen—has the greatest impact on your daily life. And by starting with the easiest spaces, you'll build up your decluttering muscle to eventually conquer even the most difficult room or category of items to minimize.

So, what do I mean by "easiest, most lived-in areas"? Well, your guest bedroom may be the easiest to declutter, but if you don't spend any time there, you won't appreciate the benefits. Likewise, you may spend the most time in your home office (up to eight hours a day, potentially), but decluttering your entire work life is typically much more difficult than minimizing the television room.

The following may not be the best order for you, depending on how you use your home. But this suggested order for minimizing your home works well because it moves from easiest to hardest, starting with the most lived-in areas:

1. **Car:** Start here. Often, in just a few minutes, you can remove everything from your car that doesn't belong. You'll feel an immediate difference the next time you step inside.

2. **Living room:** This is frequently the most lived-in space, and decluttering it can have an immediate impact on your daily life. Most families spend time in the living room every evening.

3. **Bedroom:** A calm, clutter-free bedroom promotes rest and relaxation. It might contain a few sentimental items, but not typically as much as elsewhere in the home.

4. **Bathroom:** This is usually a smaller space, making it easier to tackle.

5. **Clothes closet:** Clothing can be emotional, but making progress here changes every morning and evening routine.

6. **Kitchen:** While this space can be overwhelming, focusing on one drawer or cabinet at a time helps.

7. **Kids' areas:** These spaces often require patience, flexibility, and your children's involvement. Setting physical boundaries for toys, crafts, and so on is a helpful tool.

8. **Home office:** This is often a challenging area because of the amount of paper involved, which is why it falls later in the "easiest-to-hardest, most lived-in first" approach.

9. **Basement, attic, garage:** These are the types of spaces to leave until the very end. Generally speaking, we don't tend to spend a lot of time hanging out in them, and they can house some of the most emotionally difficult things to remove.

As you declutter, you'll notice something remarkable: Each small win builds momentum. Spending time in decluttered spaces helps you appreciate the changes taking place in your home and will motivate you to continue, eventually decluttering the hardest of spaces (think attic, basement, garage, boxes of photos, etc.).

Clearing off a countertop, organizing a drawer, or donating a box of unused items might seem insignificant, but these small steps add up. They create a sense of forward movement, which is incredibly motivating.

Step 5: Notice and articulate the practical benefits of owning less.

As you declutter, it's important to pause and reflect on the positive changes you're experiencing. By noticing and articulating these benefits, you'll reinforce your motivation and deepen your commitment to minimalism.

Dawson Trotman, founder of The Navigators, is credited with saying, "Thoughts disentangle themselves when they pass through the lips and fingertips." So, when I say, "Articulate the benefits of owning less," I genuinely mean it.

As you make progress decluttering your home, say aloud or write down every time you notice a benefit occurring. It can range from something simple like "This shelf is easier to dust" or "Putting these dishes away is easier now" to something more complex like "My children are seeing a brand-new side of me" or "I am discovering new ways to use my time and money." But every time we articulate a practical benefit of how minimalism is changing our lives, we become more inclined to keep working at it.

Here are some ways to further your resolve in minimalism:

- **Spend time in your decluttered spaces.** After decluttering a room, take a few moments to sit in it. Notice how it feels. Is it calmer? More inviting? Do you feel less stressed or more focused? Pay attention to the emotional and practical shifts. Even ask your spouse how the new room feels to them.
- **Journal your observations.** Write down what you're noticing. For example, "I love how easy it is to find my keys now" or "I feel so much more relaxed in my bedroom." Writing these reflections will help you internalize the benefits of minimalism. Or, at the very least, say them out loud to yourself or your spouse.
- **Share your wins.** Talk about your progress with a friend or family member. Sharing your experiences not only

> reinforces the positive changes but also inspires others to consider their own relationships with possessions. One of the most motivating conversations you can ever have is to tell your friend about the progress you are making at home and to hear them say, "You know, I need to do the same thing in my home." And trust me, that's a response you'll hear more times than you think.

Over time, these small observations add up and will help you more than you know.

Step 6: Establish clutter-free habits.

Decluttering your home is great, but maintaining a clutter-free lifestyle is even better. This will require intentional habits.

Steps 6 and 7 are about creating routines that help you sustain the progress you've made and prevent clutter from creeping back in. It's one thing to go on a diet and lose a bunch of weight; it's another thing to change your eating habits going forward to keep the weight from returning. That is what these final steps are all about.

To keep your home decluttered, two key clutter-free habits are worth working on: embracing regular decluttering habits and overcoming consumerism.

Embrace daily, weekly, seasonal, and annual decluttering habits

Any home that is lived in will naturally accumulate items over time. Especially with a family, it is virtually impossible to keep things from entering the home. The problems arise when we don't also have regular routines to remove items.

To keep clutter down, you'll want to learn and study the

rhythms of your home, trying to learn which clutter-free habits need to be applied daily, weekly, or seasonally.

Here's what I mean:

- **Daily habits:** These are the small, consistent actions that keep your home tidy and functional. Clutter attracts clutter, so learning which spaces in your home require daily attention is transformational. Examples include tidying up the living room every evening, cleaning the kitchen after meals, picking up clothes at the end of the day, and clearing off the bathroom counter before bed. These habits take just a few minutes but make a big difference in maintaining order.
- **Weekly habits:** Next, some things don't require daily attention but should happen weekly. Taking out the trash is the best example. But there are other slightly larger tasks, like doing laundry or sorting through mail, the fridge, your desktop, or even your email inbox. These habits help prevent small messes from becoming big problems.
- **Seasonal habits:** As the seasons change, so do our needs. Use these transitions as opportunities to reassess your possessions. For example, at the end of winter, go through your coats and boots to see what you no longer need. When school ends, declutter your kids' backpacks and school supplies. Now that my kids are in college, there are seasonal swings that happen when they return home for the summer or leave in the fall.
- **Annual habits:** Once a year, tackle larger decluttering projects, like clearing out the garage, organizing storage spaces, holding a garage sale, or decluttering your pantry.

What regular decluttering habits do you need to embrace to keep your spaces functional and peaceful? The more progress you make decluttering, the clearer these will become.

Overcome consumerism

We live in a world filled with empty consumeristic promises that bombard our senses incessantly—even within the comforts of our homes. And more than we realize, these messages begin to shape our conscious and subconscious thoughts.

As a result, too often we buy stuff we don't need. Our lives soon become buried under everything we own. And unless we learn to overcome consumerism, our homes will fill back up, and we'll lose all the spiritual benefits we sought to experience.

To counter consumerism, I want to offer a simple, life-transforming question—five simple words to ask before making any purchase:

But what if I don't?

Whenever you feel the pull of consumerism, simply ask yourself the shortened version of this thought: *What could I do if I don't make this purchase?*

Every purchase contains an opportunity cost. The question "But what if I don't?" forces us to recognize and articulate it. For example:

- If I don't buy that large-screen television, how much debt could I pay off?
- If I don't buy the bigger house, how much more money could we donate to our church?
- If I don't go clothes shopping today, how could I build up an emergency fund?
- If I don't make this purchase on Amazon, what memorable experience could I share with my family?

You know what you've been promised if you buy . . . but what if you *don't* buy it? How would your life improve if you said no?

With every purchase we make, we sacrifice a small amount of freedom. This one simple question helps us recognize exactly what that sacrifice is.

Step 7: Experiment with less.

As I mentioned earlier, Maya Angelou is credited with saying, "We need much less than we think we need." The final step in the Becker Method is about learning that truth by embracing a mindset of curiosity and exploration.

Minimalism isn't a one-time event; it's an ongoing journey of discovering how little we actually need to live a fulfilling life. This step encourages you to experiment with owning less and to challenge your assumptions about what's truly essential.

Why experiment with less?

Most of us have lived our entire lives with too much stuff—too many clothes, too many dishes, too many decorations, too much house. The world has conditioned us to believe that more is better, but minimalism invites us to question that assumption.

Experimenting with less is how we learn what's enough. It's how we answer questions like these:

- How many pairs of socks should I own?
- How many coffee mugs do I really need?
- How much Tupperware is enough?
- How many decorations make my home feel inviting without feeling cluttered?

By testing out fewer possessions, we challenge our assumptions and discover that we need much less than we think. Experimenting with less is the only pathway to truly knowing how much of anything we need—and when too much is detrimental to our potential.

How to experiment with less

Here's how to approach this step:

1. **Choose a category.** Start with one category of items in your home. It can be anything: clothing, televisions, furniture, decorations, Tupperware, books.

2. **Set a time frame for the experiment.** I recommend experimenting for twenty-nine days. This gives you enough time to adjust to the new amount and evaluate how it feels.

3. **Limit your possessions.** Reduce the items in that category to a number that feels challenging but manageable. For example, commit to wearing just thirty-three items of clothing for the next thirty-three days. Or attempt to use only one coffee mug for the next month. Or put all the televisions in your basement for the summer. Really challenge yourself on this step.

4. **Reflect and adjust.** At the end of the designated time frame, ask yourself, *What did I learn about myself? Did my life improve with no television? Was living with thirty-three articles of clothing easier or harder than I thought? Did this new amount improve my life or detract from it?* Then keep the new amount or adjust as necessary.

This experiment is always a win-win opportunity. Each time we do it, we learn something new about ourselves and our homes.

Experimenting with less isn't just about decluttering; it's

about discovering the optimal quantity of possessions for your life. Over time, these experiments will reveal that you need far less than you think—and that owning less will free your heart and soul for greater pursuits than material possessions.

For more practical guidelines about minimalism, see my book *The Minimalist Home.*

acknowledgments

As is always the case, more people than I could possibly name here deserve my gratitude for the writing of *Uncluttered Faith*. But near the top of the list are my wife, Kim; my kids, Salem and Alexa; my writing partner, Eric Stanford; my editor, Susan Tjaden and the entire team at WaterBrook / Penguin Random House; and my agent, Christopher Ferebee.

But more than anyone else, I would like to acknowledge and lift up my Lord and Savior, Jesus Christ.

When I was still a sinner and at enmity with God, Jesus did not consider equality with God something to be used to His own advantage. Instead, He made Himself nothing and took on the very nature of a servant. Motivated by love and for the sake of my eternal soul, He humbled Himself by becoming obedient to death—even death on a cross!

His resurrection three days later destroyed death and brought life and immortality to light through the gospel. After this holy and eternal priest had offered a pleasing sacrifice for my sins and purchased redemption, He sat down at the right hand of God as an advocate on my behalf.

But His work in my life was not complete. For how could I call on the One I didn't believe in? How could I believe if I had not heard? And how could I hear without someone preaching to me? So, this glorious Jesus did not leave me on my own but sent workers into the harvest field of my life with the good news of the gospel.

While I was dead in my transgressions and sins, He saved my life and soul. It was by grace through faith that I was saved—not through my own efforts but by trusting alone in the finished work of Jesus. Salvation is found in no one else, for there is no other name under heaven given to mankind by which we must be saved.

Years later, while living for my own self-interest, God changed me through the voice of His Holy Spirit, again lifting up for me the person of Jesus Christ. Because of God's great mercy, I offered myself as a living sacrifice.

From that moment on—a decision I have never regretted—Jesus has been the only true source of joy, meaning, and purpose in my life. He gifted me and called me. He prepared a good work for me to accomplish. And this book, to the very best of my ability, was written to fulfill that call.

May Jesus Christ, above all else, forever be acknowledged and glorified in my life and work.

notes

Chapter 1: The Way to Unlock God's Blessings

1. A few stories in the book contain composite characters, and some names have been changed to protect privacy.
2. Joshua Becker, "Minimalism Introduces Us to Intentionality," Becoming Minimalist, accessed May 6, 2025, www.becomingminimalist.com/minimalism-introduces-intentionality/.

Chapter 2: The Culture We Are Swimming In

1. "The Rise of American Consumerism," *American Experience*, accessed May 13, 2025, www.pbs.org/wgbh/americanexperience/features/tupperware-consumer.
2. Evan Comen, "The Size of a Home the Year You Were Born," 24/7 Wall St., updated December 20, 2021, https://247wallst.com/special-report/2016/05/25/the-size-of-a-home-the-year-you-were-born/; *Quarterly Starts and Completions by Purpose and Design* (U.S. Census Bureau and U.S. Department of Housing and Urban Development, New Residential Construction, February 19, 2025), table Q1, www.census.gov/construction/nrc/pdf/quarterly_starts_completions.pdf.
3. David McMillin, "How Big of a House Do You Really Need? How Home Sizes Have Evolved over Time," Bankrate, June 17, 2025, www.bankrate.com/real-estate/average-home-size.
4. Mary MacVean, "For Many People, Gathering Possessions Is Just the Stuff of Life," *Los Angeles Times,* March 21, 2014, www.latimes

.com/health/la-he-keeping-stuff-20140322-story.html. This figure could probably use some updating. But undoubtedly there are at least tens of thousands of items in most U.S. homes.

5. Al Harris, "U.S. Self-Storage Industry Statistics," SpareFoot, updated October 10, 2024, http://sparefootblogs.wpengine.com/blog/self-storage-industry-statistics.
6. Mirela Mohan, "More than a Third of Americans Rent Self Storage, with Furniture the Most Stored Item," StorageCafe, August 15, 2022, www.storagecafe.com/blog/self-storage-use-and-main-demand-drivers.
7. "Take Back Your Garage: American Garages Store More Clutter than Cars, According to Craftsman Survey," PR Newswire, November 1, 2022, www.prnewswire.com/news-releases/take-back-your-garage-american-garages-store-more-clutter-than-cars-according-to-craftsman-survey-301664129.html.
8. "Lost and Found: The Average American Spends 2.5 Days Each Year Looking for Lost Items Collectively Costing U.S. Households $2.7 Billion Annually in Replacement Costs," PR Newswire, May 2, 2017, emphasis added, www.prnewswire.com/news-releases/lost-and-found-the-average-american-spends-25-days-each-year-looking-for-lost-items-collectively-costing-us-households-27-billion-annually-in-replacement-costs-300449305.html.
9. Kathryn Horvath, "How Many Clothes Are Too Many?" PIRG, May 10, 2024, https://pirg.org/articles/how-many-clothes-are-too-many.
10. Dana Thomas, "The High Price of Fast Fashion," *Wall Street Journal*, April 29, 2019, www.wsj.com/articles/the-high-price-of-fast-fashion-11567096637.
11. Marjorie van Elven, "People Do Not Wear at Least 50 Percent of Their Wardrobes, Says Study," FashionUnited, August 16, 2018, https://fashionunited.uk/news/fashion/people-do-not-wear-at-least-50-percent-of-their-wardrobes-according-to-study/2018081638356.
12. van Elven, "People Do Not Wear."
13. "House Size by Country 2025," World Population Review, accessed May 14, 2025, https://worldpopulationreview.com/country-rankings/house-size-by-country.
14. Tamara E. Holmes, "Americans Spend $18,000 Per Year on Non-Essentials," Yahoo! Finance, May 6, 2019, https://finance.yahoo.com/news/americans-spend-18-000-per-153406769.html.

15. "Buyer's Remorse Due to Online Shopping Has Affected Seventy-four Percent of Americans, According to Survey Commissioned by Slickdeals," PR Newswire, March 28, 2022, www.prnewswire.com/news-releases/buyers-remorse-due-to-online-shopping-has-affected-seventy-four-percent-of-americans-according-to-survey-commissioned-by-slickdeals-301511257.html.
16. "Study Reveals Clutter Epidemic Cause: 'Low Sell-Esteem,'" PR Newswire, March 19, 2019, www.prnewswire.com/news-releases/study-reveals-clutter-epidemic-cause-low-sell-esteem-300814777.html.
17. Matt Schulz, "2025 Credit Card Debt Statistics," LendingTree, updated June 5, 2025, www.lendingtree.com/credit-cards/study/credit-card-debt-statistics/.
18. Jack Caporal, "Average American Household Debt in 2025: Facts and Figures," Motley Fool Money, updated May 14, 2025, www.fool.com/money/research/average-household-debt.
19. Caleb Silver, "The Top 25 Economies in the World," Investopedia, updated January 29, 2025, www.investopedia.com/insights/worlds-top-economies/.
20. Phillip Ozimek et al., "Materialism in Social Media—More Social Media Addiction and Stress Symptoms, Less Satisfaction with Life," *Telematics and Informatics Reports* 13 (March 2024): 100117, https://doi.org/10.1016/j.teler.2024.100117.
21. Olaya Moldes et al., "Has the COVID-19 Pandemic Made Us More Materialistic?: The Effect of COVID-19 and Lockdown Restrictions on the Endorsement of Materialism," *Psychology & Marketing* 39, no. 5 (2022): 892–905. https://doi.org/10.1002/mar.21627.
22. James E. Burroughs and Aric Rindfleisch, "Materialism and Well-Being: A Conflicting Values Perspective," *Journal of Consumer Research* 29, no. 3 (2002): 348–70, https://doi.org/10.1086/344429. Another study suggests that cultural Christians tend to be more involved in consumerism and materialism than people who profess a devout inner faith in Christ. Jaskaran Singh et al., "Religious Influences in Unrestrained Consumer Behaviour," *Journal of Retailing and Consumer Services* 58 (January 2021): 102262, https://doi.org/10.1016/j.jretconser.2020.102262.
23. Peter Mundey, *Sacred Consumption: The Religions of Christianity and Consumerism in America* (Lexington, 2023), 2.

24. Denni Arli et al., "The Effect of Religiosity on Luxury Goods: The Case of Chilean Youths," *International Journal of Consumer Studies* 44, no. 3 (2020): 181–90, https://doi.org/10.1111/ijcs.12559.
25. Randy Alcorn, *Money, Possessions, and Eternity* (Tyndale, 2003), 48.

Chapter 3: True Abundance

1. Quoted in Elisabeth Elliot, *Shadow of the Almighty: The Life and Testament of Jim Elliot* (Zondervan, 1958), 15.
2. Tim Kasser, "What Psychology Says About Materialism and the Holidays," interview by American Psychological Association, 2014, www.apa.org/news/press/releases/2014/12/materialism-holidays.
3. Joshua N. Hook et al., "Minimalism, Voluntary Simplicity, and Well-Being: A Systematic Review of the Empirical Literature," *The Journal of Positive Psychology* 18, no. 1 (2023): 130–41.
4. Amy Isham et al., "The Problematic Role of Materialistic Values in the Pursuit of Sustainable Well-Being," *International Journal of Environmental Research and Public Health* 19, no. 6 (2022): 3673, https://doi.org/10.3390/ijerph19063673.
5. Jim Murphy, *Inner Excellence: Train Your Mind for Extraordinary Performance and the Best Possible Life,* rev. ed. (Academy of Excellence, 2020), xii, emphasis added. In Murphy's book, "really" is italicized.

Chapter 4: Unmasking Your Heart's True Desires

1. Marsha L. Richins and Scott Dawson, "A Consumer Values Orientation for Materialism and Its Measurement: Scale Development and Validation," *Journal of Consumer Research* 19, no. 3 (1992): 303–16, https://doi.org/10.1086/209304.

Chapter 5: Closer to Jesus

1. "Take Less. Do More.," Glen Van Peski, accessed May 19, 2025, www.glenvanpeski.com/book/take-less-do-more/.
2. Glen Van Peski, email message with the author, November 4, 2024. See also Glen Van Peski, *Take Less. Do More.: Surprising Life Lessons in Generosity, Gratitude, and Curiosity from an Ultralight Backpacker* (Forefront Books, 2024).
3. Van Peski, *Take Less. Do More.*, introduction.

4. Randy Alcorn, "Our Skewed View of Wealth," Eternal Perspective Ministries, May 1, 2024, www.epm.org/resources/2024/May/1/skewed-view-wealth.
5. Richard J. Foster, *Celebration of Discipline: The Path to Spiritual Growth,* special anniversary edition (HarperOne, 2018), 83.
6. "How Rich Am I?," Giving What We Can, accessed May 19, 2025, www.givingwhatwecan.org/how-rich-am-i.
7. Marta Schoch et al., "Half of the Global Population Lives on Less than US$6.85 Per Person Per Day," *Let's Talk Development* (blog), World Bank Blogs, December 8, 2022, https://blogs.worldbank.org/en/developmenttalk/half-global-population-lives-less-us685-person-day.

Chapter 6: A Life Without Greed

1. Maria Das Neves Severo de Lira et al., "Dispositional Greed and Life Satisfaction: The Role of Social Comparison for Well-Being," *Psychological Health Medicine* 29, no. 8 (2024): 1425–36, https://pubmed.ncbi.nlm.nih.gov/38498980.
2. Hiranmayi Srinivasan and Amanda Morelli, "The American Dream Now Costs $4.4 Million," Investopedia, September 4, 2024, www.investopedia.com/cost-of-the-american-dream-2024-8705906.
3. Srinivasan and Morelli, "American Dream."
4. "Alan and Katherine Barnhart," video interview, Generous Giving, accessed May 20, 2025, https://generousgiving.org/alan-and-katherine-barnhart/; Liz Essley Whyte, "Giving It All," *Philanthropy Roundtable,* Spring 2014, www.philanthropyroundtable.org/magazine/spring-2014-giving-it-all.
5. "Alan and Katherine Barnhart."
6. "Alan and Katherine Barnhart."
7. Whyte, "Giving It All."
8. "Alan and Katherine Barnhart."
9. Timothy Keller, *Counterfeit Gods: The Empty Promises of Money, Sex, and Power, and the Only Hope That Matters* (Dutton, 2009), 53.

Chapter 7: The End of Anxiety

1. Tori DeAngelis, "Consumerism and Its Discontents," *Monitor on Psychology* 35, no. 6 (2004): 52, www.apa.org/monitor/jun04/discontents.

2. Zoë Kim, *Minimalism for Families: Practical Minimalist Living Strategies to Simplify Your Home and Life* (Althea Press, 2017), 14.

Chapter 8: Living on Purpose

1. Jason Fernando, "Opportunity Cost: Definition, Formula, and Examples," Investopedia, updated May 31, 2025, www.investopedia.com/terms/o/opportunitycost.asp.
2. Kelvin Wong, "Should I Have Another Slice of Cheesecake? A Basic Lesson in Economics," *Simplify Magazine*, September 2018, 51–59, https://simplifymagazine.com/essay/economics/.
3. *Thayer's Greek Lexicon*, "1805. *exagorazó*," Bible Hub, accessed May 21, 2025, https://biblehub.com/greek/1805.htm.
4. Jack Kornfield, *Buddha's Little Instruction Book* (Bantam, 1994), 39.
5. This wording is from the 1984 edition of the New International Version.
6. Again, this is from the NIV 1984 edition.

Chapter 9: Room to Grow

1. Patrick Van Kessel, "How Americans Feel About the Satisfactions and Stresses of Modern Life," Pew Research Center, February 5, 2020, www.pewresearch.org/short-reads/2020/02/05/how-americans-feel-about-the-satisfactions-and-stresses-of-modern-life/.
2. Esteban Ortiz-Ospina et al., "Time Use," Our World in Data, updated February 2024, https://ourworldindata.org/time-use.
3. "Christians," Religious Landscape Study, Pew Research Center, accessed May 22, 2025, www.pewresearch.org/religious-landscape-study/christians/christian; Gregory A. Smith et al., *Decline of Christianity in the U.S. Has Slowed, May Have Leveled Off* (Pew Research Center, 2025), 186, www.pewresearch.org/wp-content/uploads/sites/20/2025/02/PR_2025.02.26_religious-landscape-study_report.pdf.
4. Jeffery Fulks et al., *State of the Bible USA 2022* (American Bible Society, 2022), x, https://1s712.americanbible.org/state-of-the-bible/stateofthebible/State_of_the_bible-2022.pdf.
5. "Christians," Religious Landscape Study; Smith, *Decline of Christianity*, 183–85.

6. Ann McNeals, "We Asked 7,454 Christians How Often They Pray . . . and the Results Were Surprising," Grace & Prayers, accessed May 22, 2025, https://graceandprayers.com/christian-prayer-frequency-statistics.
7. Heidi Deddens, "Minimalism and Monasticism," *Comment* magazine, December 3, 2018, https://comment.org/minimalism-and-monasticism.
8. Sue Shellenbarger, "Why You Can't Concentrate at Work," *The Wall Street Journal*, May 9, 2017, www.wsj.com/articles/why-you-cant-concentrate-at-work-1494342840; Lucy Erickson, "Visual 'Noise,' Distractibility, and Classroom Design," The Learning Scientists, September 20, 2017, https://www.learningscientists.org/blog/2017/9/20-1; and Jun Xie et al., "The Role of Visual Noise in Influencing Mental Load and Fatigue in a Steady-State Motion Visual Evoked Potential-Based Brain-Computer Interface," *Sensors* 17, no. 8 (2017): 1873, www.mdpi.com/1424-8220/17/8/1873.
9. Associated Press, "Picture This: More TVs Now than People in Typical Home," *Los Angeles Daily News*, updated August 29, 2017, www.dailynews.com/2006/09/22/picture-this-more-tvs-now-than-people-in-typical-home.
10. Annie Eisner, "Why Decluttering Is a Spiritual Practice (and How to Start)," *Relevant* magazine, October 3, 2024, https://relevantmagazine.com/culture/why-decluttering-is-a-spiritual-practice-and-how-to-start.

Chapter 10: People over Possessions

1. For some of the Bible's many powerful passages on relationship, see these: Matthew 18:15; John 13:14–15, 34–35; Romans 12:13, 18; Galatians 6:1; Ephesians 4:2, 15, 29, 32; 1 Thessalonians 5:11; Hebrews 10:24–25; James 1:19–20; 1 Peter 4:9; and 1 John 4:7.
2. Rik Pieters, "Bidirectional Dynamics of Materialism and Loneliness: Not Just a Vicious Cycle," *Journal of Consumer Research* 40, no. 4 (2013): 615–31, doi.org/10.1086/671564.
3. Caroline Rogers and Rona Hart, "Home and the Extended-Self: Exploring Associations Between Clutter and Wellbeing," *Journal of Environmental Psychology* 73 (2021), https://doi.org/10.1016/j.jenvp.2021.101553.
4. Darby E. Saxbe and Rena Repetti, "No Place Like Home: Home

Tours Correlate with Daily Patterns of Mood and Cortisol," *Personality and Social Psychology Bulletin* 36, no. 1 (2010): 71–81, https://doi.org/10.1177/0146167209352864.

5. Libby Sander, "Time for a Kondo Clean-Out? Here's What Clutter Does to Your Brain and Body," *The Conversation*, January 20, 2019, https://theconversation.com/time-for-a-kondo-clean-out-heres-what-clutter-does-to-your-brain-and-body-109947; Eleesha Lockett, "Emotional Signs of Too Much Stress," *Healthline*, updated January 22, 2025, https://www.healthline.com/health/emotional-symptoms-of-stress; Hope Gillette, "What Are the Behavioral Symptoms of Stress?," *Healthline*, September 26, 2023, https://www.healthline.com/health/stress/behavioral-symptoms-of-stress.
6. Tony Buchanan, "How Stress Is Contagious," *Psychology Today*, September 22, 2023, www.psychologytoday.com/us/blog/stress-on-the-brain/202309/how-stress-is-contagious.
7. Habib Yaribeygi et al., "The Impact of Stress on Body Function: A Review," *EXCLI Journal* 16 (2017): 1057–72, https://pmc.ncbi.nlm.nih.gov/articles/PMC5579396/; Rupal Kumar et al., "Obesity and Stress: A Contingent Paralysis," *International Journal of Preventive Medicine* 13, no. 1 (2022): 95, https://pmc.ncbi.nlm.nih.gov/articles/PMC9362746/.
8. Kasey Lloyd and William Pennington, "Towards a Theory of Minimalism and Wellbeing," *International Journal of Applied Positive Psychology* 5 (2020): 121–36, https://doi.org/10.1007/s41042-020-00030-y.
9. Cindy Chan and Cassie Mogilner, "Experiential Gifts Foster Stronger Social Relationships than Material Gifts," *Journal of Consumer Research* 43, no. 6 (2017): 913–31, https://doi.org/10.1093/jcr/ucw067.
10. Bruce Feiler, *The Secrets of Happy Families: Improve Your Mornings, Tell Your Family History, Fight Smarter, Go Out and Play, and Much More* (William Morrow, 2013), 16.
11. Feiler, *Secrets of Happy Families,* 16; Elizabeth P. Parks et al., "Influence of Stress in Parents on Child Obesity and Related Behaviors," *Pediatrics* 130, no. 5 (2012): e1096–e1104, https://pmc.ncbi.nlm.nih.gov/articles/PMC3483892/; Erin Masterson and Wael Sabbah, "Maternal Allostatic Load, Caretaking Behaviors, and Child Dental Caries Experience: A Cross-Sectional Evaluation of Linked Mother-Child Data From the Third National Health and Nutrition

Examination Survey," *American Journal of Public Health* 105 (2015): 2306–11, https://doi.org/10.2105/AJPH.2015.302729.

12. Dongxu Li and Xi Guo, "The Effect of the Time Parents Spend with Children on Children's Well-Being," *Frontiers in Psychology* 14 (April 2, 2023), https://doi.org/10.3389/fpsyg.2023.1096128.
13. Jasara Hogan et al., "Time Spent Together in Intimate Relationships: Implications for Relationship Functioning," *Contemporary Family Therapy* 43, no. 3 (2021): 226–33, https://pmc.ncbi.nlm.nih.gov/articles/PMC8320759/.
14. James Baldwin, "Fifth Avenue, Uptown: A Letter from Harlem," in *Nobody Knows My Name: More Notes of a Native Son* (Dell, 1961), 59.

Chapter 11: Success Redefined

1. Tim Kizziar, quoted in Francis Chan, *Crazy Love: Overwhelmed by a Relentless God* (David C. Cook, 2013), 92.
2. C. S. Lewis, *The Weight of Glory: And Other Addresses* (1949; HarperCollins, 2001), 26.

Chapter 12: A Purpose Beyond the Paycheck

1. "One Third of Your Life Is Spent at Work," Gettysburg College, accessed May 24, 2025, www.gettysburg.edu/news/stories?id=79db7b34-630c-4f49-ad32-4ab9ea48e72b.
2. John Wesley, "The Use of Money," The Sermons of John Wesley—Sermon 50, ed. Jennette Descalzo, Wesley Center Online, 1999, https://wesley.nnu.edu/john-wesley/the-sermons-of-john-wesley-1872-edition/sermon-50-the-use-of-money.
3. Here's one example: Daniel Kahneman and Angus Deaton, "High Income Improves Evaluation of Life but Not Emotional Well-Being," *Proceedings of the National Academy of Sciences USA* 107, no. 38 (2010), 16489–93, www.pnas.org/cgi/doi/10.1073/pnas.1011492107.
4. *Memoirs of the Life of Joseph Alleine: Including a Narrative Written by His Widow, Mrs. Theodosia Alleine* (Philadelphia: American Sunday School Union, [1827?]), 155.

Chapter 13: Less Stuff, More Giving

1. "Discover Survey: Anxiety and Avoidance Are Driving the Financial Lives of Many Americans," Business Wire, July 23, 2024, www.businesswire.com/news/home/20240723820169/en/Discover-Survey-Anxiety-and-Avoidance-are-Driving-the-Financial-Lives-of-Many-Americans.
2. "Survey Reveals Majority of Americans Still Living Paycheck to Paycheck," PR Newswire, September 25, 2024, www.prnewswire.com/news-releases/survey-reveals-majority-of-americans-still-living-paycheck-to-paycheck-302257819.
3. *The Giving Gap: Changes in Evangelical Generosity,* Infinity Concepts | Grey Matter Research, 2024, www.infinityconcepts.com/wp-content/uploads/2024/09/The-Giving-Gap-Downloadable.pdf.
4. "Ninety-five percent of practicing Christians donated to charity, followed by 68% of non-practicing Christians and 51% of non-Christians. The average amount of money donated by practicing Christians amounted to $5,350. That figure dropped to $3,806 among non-practicing Christians and $3,163 among non-Christians." Ryan Foley, "Practicing Christians Give More to Charity than Non-Christians: Study," *Christian Post,* November 15, 2023, www.christianpost.com/news/practicing-christians-give-more-to-charity-than-non-christians.html.
5. Bob Lotich, "How I Made $2,145 Last Month by Decluttering," Seedtime, accessed May 25, 2025, https://seedtime.com/how-i-made-2k-decluttering.
6. Andrei Popa, "US Discretionary Spending Up: Colorado and Utah Top All Other States in Financial Well-Being," StorageCafe, September 2, 2024, www.storagecafe.com/blog/us-discretionary-spending-up-colorado-and-utah-lead-in-financial-well-being/.
7. Sabrina Karl, "Spring House Hunting in a Top 50 Metro? Here's the Average Mortgage Payment in Each One," Investopedia, April 9, 2025, www.investopedia.com/spring-house-hunting-in-a-top-50-metro-heres-the-average-mortgage-payment-in-each-one-11711798.
8. "Rent Trends in the United States," Apartments.com, updated September 2025, www.apartments.com/rent-market-trends/us.
9. Stephanie Minasian-Koncewicz, "Utility Bills 101: Average Costs of

Utility Bills by State," This Old House, updated August 12, 2025, www.thisoldhouse.com/moving/utility-bills-101.

10. Linda Bell, "Study: Owning a Home Costs over $21,000 a Year in Hidden Expenses," Bankrate, June 9, 2025, www.bankrate.com/home-equity/hidden-costs-of-homeownership-study/.
11. Juan Cruz, "Rising Homeowners Insurance Costs: Why Premiums Are Reaching Record Highs," Inszone Insurance Services, September 2, 2025, https://inszoneinsurance.com/blog/rising-homeowners-premiums.
12. Jack Caporal, "American Households' Average Monthly Expenses: $6,440," Motley Fool Money, updated July 24, 2025, www.fool.com/money/research/average-monthly-expenses.
13. "Food Waste in America in 2025," Recycle Track Systems, accessed September 11, 2025, www.rts.com/resources/guides/food-waste-america.
14. Dan Shepard and Dragana Filipovik, "149 Holiday Spending Statistics, from Valentine's Day to New Year's Eve," LendingTree, updated February 2, 2025, www.lendingtree.com/debt-consolidation/holiday-spending-statistics.
15. "Credit Market Showing Signs of Stability and Measured Growth at Mid-Point of 2025," TransUnion, August 14, 2025, https://newsroom.transunion.com/q2-2025-ciir.
16. Jennifer Taylor, "The Widow's Mite," Samford University Library, Special Collection Treasures, July 2005, https://library.samford.edu/special/treasures/2005/mite.html.
17. Elizabeth Dunn et al., "Prosocial Spending and Buying Time Money as a Tool for Increasing Subjective Well-Being," *Advances in Experimental Social Psychology* 61 (2020): 67–126, https://doi.org/10.1016/bs.aesp.2019.09.001.
18. "Giving Tuesday: 5 Health Benefits of Giving," ThinkHealth, November 12, 2021, https://thinkhealth.priorityhealth.com/giving-tuesday-health-benefits-of-giving/?utm_source=chatgpt.com.
19. J. Hudson Taylor, *J. Hudson Taylor: An Autobiography* (ReadaClassic.com, 2010), 14.

Chapter 14: Enough Is Enough

1. Richard Swenson, "Contentment: The Secret of a Lasting Calm," Christian Medical & Dental Associations, *Today's Christian Doctor,* Summer 2013, https://resources.cmda.org/article/contentment-the-secret-of-a-lasting-calm.
2. "Practicing Gratitude for Better Health and Well-Being," University of Utah, November 19, 2021, https://healthcare.utah.edu/healthfeed/2021/11/practicing-gratitude-better-health-and-well-being.
3. See Philippians 3:14; Hebrews 12:1; Galatians 6:9; and Colossians 3:23.
4. See Hebrews 13:5; 1 Timothy 6:6; and Matthew 6:25.
5. Mary Ellen Edmunds, *You Can Never Get Enough of What You Don't Need: The Quest for Contentment* (Deseret Book, 2005), 186–87.

Chapter 15: More than Happy

1. "Vocab Insight: Mammon / Wealth," BibleProject, accessed May 25, 2025, https://bibleproject.com/videos/vocab-insight-mammon-wealth/.
2. Ed Diener et al., "Beyond the Hedonic Treadmill: Revising the Adaptation Theory of Well-Being," *American Psychology* 61, no. 4 (2006): 305–14, http://doi.org/10.1037/0003-066X.61.4.305.
3. Will Kenton, "Lifestyle Inflation: What It Is, How It Works, and Example," Investopedia, updated May 17, 2025, www.investopedia.com/terms/l/lifestyle-inflation.asp.
4. When we moved to Arizona, we downsized on purpose, getting a three-bedroom, two-bathroom house of 1,700 square feet—smaller than the first home we bought years earlier.
5. Here is the full quote: "Their knowledge will increase to eternity; and if their knowledge, doubtless their holiness. For as they increase in the knowledge of God and of the works of God, the more they will see of his excellency; and the more they see of his excellency . . . the more will they love him; and the more they love God, *the more delight and happiness . . . will they have in him.*" Jonathan Edwards, *The "Miscellanies": (Entry Nos. a–z, aa–zz, 1–500)*, ed. Thomas A. Schafer, in The Works of Jonathan Edwards 13 (Yale University Press, 1994), 275–76, emphasis added.
6. Oswald Chambers, "August 31: My Joy . . . Your Joy," *My Utmost for*

His Highest, Classic Edition, accessed May 26, 2025, https://utmost.org/classic/my-joy-your-joy-classic.

Chapter 16: Shine a Brighter Light

1. A. W. Tozer, *The Pursuit of God* (Moody Publishers, 2006), 70.

Bonus: The Becker Method

1. Teresa Amabile and Steven Kramer, *The Progress Principle: Using Small Wins to Ignite Joy, Engagement, and Productivity at Work* (Harvard Business Review Press, 2011).

about the author

Joshua Becker holds a master's degree in theological studies from Bethel Seminary. He served as an ordained pastor for fifteen years in the Christian and Missionary Alliance at churches in Wisconsin, Vermont, and Arizona.

He is also the bestselling author of *Things That Matter, The Minimalist Home, The More of Less, Simplify*, and *Clutterfree with Kids*.

He is the founder and editor of Becoming Minimalist (www.becomingminimalist.com), a website dedicated to intentional living visited by 1 million readers every month, with a social media following of more than 4 million. His blog was named by *SUCCESS* magazine as one of the top ten personal-development websites on the internet, and his writing has been featured in publications all around the world.

He is the creator of *Simplify Magazine* and *Simple Money Magazine* and a contributing writer for *Forbes*.

Joshua and his young family were introduced to minimalism during a short conversation with their neighbor in 2008. Since then, Joshua's story and writing have inspired millions around the world to find more life by owning fewer possessions. Today, based on his thoughtful and intentional approach to minimalism, he is one of the leading voices in the modern simplicity movement.

He is also the founder of The Hope Effect, a nonprofit organization changing how the world cares for orphans.

His online course, Uncluttered, has helped more than ninety thousand people declutter their homes and live more intentional lives focused on the things that matter most. His app, Clutterfree, is the only app to create a personalized, room-by-room decluttering to-do list for an individual's home. And his YouTube channel is followed by hundreds of thousands.

Joshua lives in Peoria, Arizona, with his wife and two teenage kids.

Visit his website: www.joshuabecker.com.

Becoming Minimalist *inspires us to live more by owning less. The website is home to over 1 million readers per month who recognize life is too valuable to waste when we chase material possessions.*

With encouragement, inspiration, and practical advice, it helps us to discover the life-giving benefits of owning less.

OTHER RESOURCES:

YouTube: Hundreds of free videos to help you remove distractions and live a more intentional life. Learn more at youtube.com/c/joshuabecker.

The Clutterfree App: The first and only handheld app to create a personalized, step-by-step road map to declutter your home. Track your progress, find inspiration, complete challenges, and discover specific bonus plans for your home's toughest decluttering spaces. Available for download on the App Store and Google Play Store.

Simplify Magazine: A quarterly digital publication that pulls together experts in various fields to address some of the most pressing needs of the modern family. Find out more at simplifymagazine.com.

Becker Method Certified Professionals: In a world saturated with excess stuff, it's easy to miss what really matters. A Becker Method certified expert can clear the clutter and focus you on what's important. Make the choice—start living the life you want today. Learn more at https://beckermethodcertified.com/find-a-pro.

THE HOPE EFFECT: As mentioned in *Things That Matter*, this nonprofit organization founded by Joshua and Kim Becker is changing the way the world cares for orphans—because every child deserves a family. You can join the cause at hopeeffect.com.